PERSPECTIVE OF BUDDHIST STUDIES

(Giuseppe Tucci Birth Centenary Volume)

Indo-Tibetan Studies Series

Editor of the Series
Narendra Kumar Dash

Volume I : edited by Dr. N.K. Dash
Tibetan Studies: Past and Present

Volume II : edited by Prof. Pranabananda Jash
Perspective of Buddhist Studies
(Giuseppe Tucci Birth Centenary Volume)

Indo-Tibetan Studies Series-II

Perspective of Buddhist Studies

(Giuseppe Tucci Birth Centenary Volume)

Edited by

Pranabananda Jash

Kaveri Books
New Delhi-110 002

ISBN - 978-81-74790-46-0

Edition 2017

Published by
Kaveri Books
4832/24, Ansari Road
New Delhi-110002 (India)
Tel: 011-23288140, 23245799
E-mail : kaveribooks@vsnl.com
kaveribooks@gmail.com
Website: www.kaveribooks.com

Typeset at
Delta Book World, New Delhi - 110 002

PRINTED IN INDIA

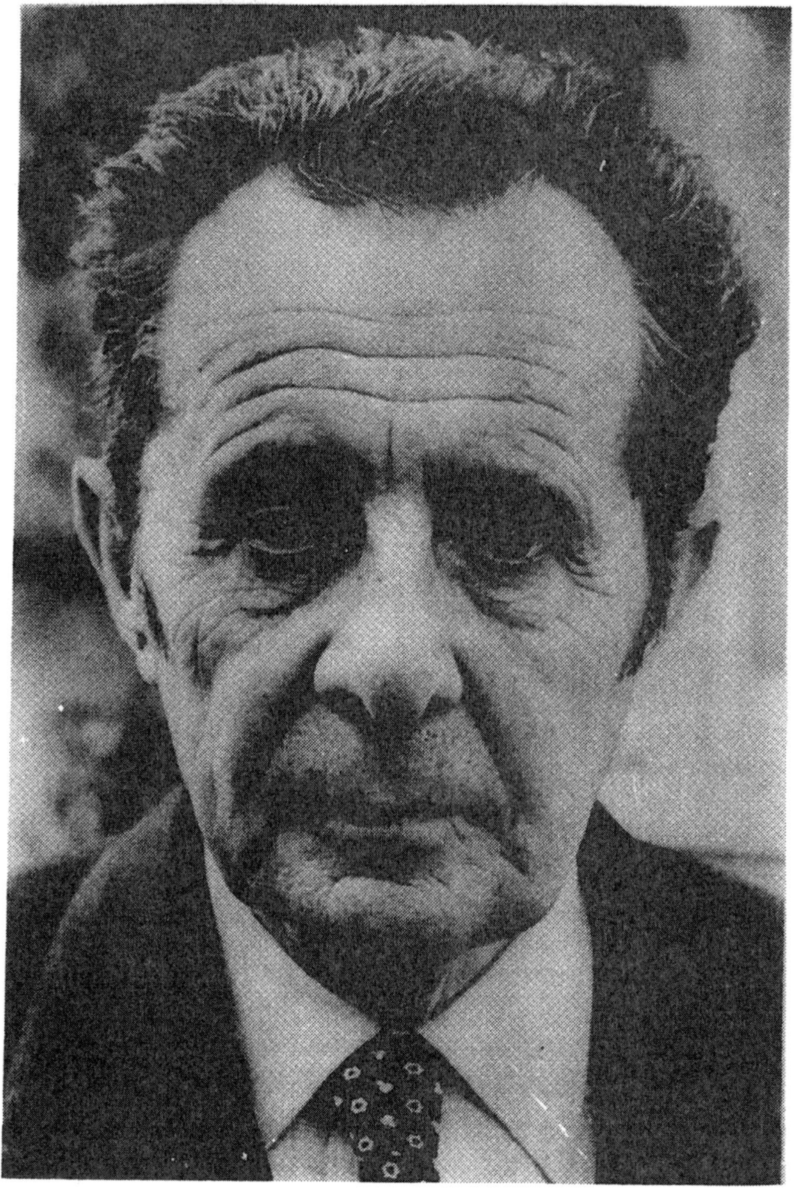

Prof. Giuseppe Tucci
(b. June 05, 1894, d. April 05, 1984)

VISVA-BHARATI

FOUNDED BY

RABINDRANATH TAGORE

ACHARYA
INDER KUMAR GUJARAL
UPACHARYA
DILIP KUMAR SINHA

• विश्वभारती •
शान्तिनिकेतन

SANTINIKETAN—731 235
WEST BENGAL, INDIA

Prologue

It gives me great pleasure to bring out the Second Volume of the Indo-Tibetan Studies Series-II within the short span of time. This Volume is dedicated to the great Indologist Professor Giuseppe Tucci, an outstanding scholar of oriental studies. A prolific writer, Dr. Tucci never confined his area of studies within a particular discipline, but he expressed his thoughts and ideas through various dimensions as it is recorded and analysed in different papers of this Volume. I am thankful to the convenor of the conference, Professor Pranabananda Jash and contributors for their scholarly papers on Tucci and his writings.

N Dash

Narendra Kumar Dash

Chairman, Department of Indo-Tibetan Studies

Contents

Editorial

At the outset I must confess that the present volume was scheduled to be published a couple of years back, but of circumstances beyond control delayed the publication. I sincerely regret the delay.

An outstanding scholar of global reputation, Giuseppe Tucci (b. June 5, 1894 d. April 5, 1984) visited Santiniketan as early as 1925 to teach Italian, Chinese and Tibetan in the Vidya-Bhavana, Visva-Bharati. Apart from his academic achievements he played a vital role in building a bridge of culture between the East and West.

To commemorate the birth centenary of this eminent Italian Orientalist as well as to evaluate his academic works, Visva-Bharati decided to organise a national conference or seminar at Santiniketan. In fact, the main objective in holding the seminar was thus to provide a National Forum to scholars from different Institutions and Universities for discussing the stupenduous contributions of Professor Tucci in the field of oriental studies. The Seminar was held from 3rd-4th September, 1994. There were altogether nineteen participants with their research papers, but the papers which were not resubmitted after revision could not be incorporated in this volume. On the other hand, three papers which were not physically presented in the Seminar have been included in order to cover a wide spectrum of research studies envisaged by Professor Tucci.

Professor Tucci possessed a rare quality of pursuing any kind of research investigation, however painstaking, in quest of knowledge for oriental studies. All his publications bear a stamp on meticulous scholarship, original knowledge of exploratory outcome dealing with source materials and a rare breadth of perspective. The corpus of his research activities numbering no less than thirty books and three hundred papers on different facets of history, archaeology, religion especially Buddhism and culture of Indian sub-continent evoke our admiration. To analyse the subject properly with adequate justification, he learnt various classical languages like Sanskrit, Greek, Latin, Persian, Tibetan, Chinese, Italian, Bengali, etc. One can easily realize the vastness of his knowledge if one makes an assessment of his two volumes, viz. *Storia della Filosofia Indiana* (1957) and the *Ancient Civilization of Transhimalaya*, which is an English translation of Tibet, both published in 1993. Moreover, the foundation of the *Institute Italiano per il Medio ed Estremo Oriente*, widely known as ISMEO in 1933 is an indelible mark in the domain of oriental studies.

A glimpse into the content of the present volume will bring into focus the impact of Professor Tucci on the succeeding generation of research scholars working in the field of Oriental/ Indological studies. I am happy to be able to bring out the seminar proceeding in print, but I am at the same time, deeply shocked to record the sad demise of two of our distinguished scholars - Professor R.S.Tomar and Professor M.S. Mallick, who could not go through their writings in print. Nevertheless, it gives me immense pleasure to express my thanks to all the contributors of the volume. The Publisher Mr. Rakesh Goel and his team of the Kaveri Books, New Delhi, deserve my sincere thanks for printing and publishing it within a very short time. I am also thankful to Mr. Jayanta Chowdhury and his associates of the U-Compute, Bolpur to prepare the Press Copy of the present volume.

Pranabananda Jash

Inaugural Address at the Conference on Professor Giuseppe Tucci

1

Sabyasachi Bhattacharya

In one of his lesser known essays, Karl Popper compares human civilization to a conversation. "As civilised human beings, we are the inheritors... of a conversation begun in the primeval forests and made more articulate in the course of the centuries.... Properly speaking it is impossible in the absence of diversity of voices: in it different universes of discourse meet, acknowledge each other and enjoy an oblique relationship which neither requires nor forecasts their being assimilated to one another." (K. Popper, *The voice of poetry in the conversation of mankind*, London, 1959, p.10-11). This interesting imagery of the human civilization as a conversation leads one to reflect upon the fact that in this conversation the individual voice of India was not heard for many centuries until the late 19th and early 20th centuries. In making it heard, the Orientalists of Europe played a role. Some of these Orientalists were attracted by the genius of Tagore and by his effort to build at Santiniketan an institution which, in its own way, tried to make this conversation between different cultures possible. One such European scholar was Giuseppe Tucci.

To locate Tucci in the Orientalists' historiographic tradition and, secondly, to understand the possibilites and limits of the cultural encounters that took place in his times in Santiniketan - these are two essential tasks before us today.

As regards the first, it is not just a matter of aggregating the technical contribution and information accumulated by the labour of Professor Tucci and his peers in the field of Oriental Studies in Europe. As you know, the term Orientalist has been of late, a term of opprobrium. In the last two decades, particularly since Edward Said in his work on Orientalism has condemned European Orientalists' Eurocentric bias, it is customary to look askance at the historiographic role of the Orientalists. I think it will be a mistake to lump together all of European perception of Asia under a blanket category, Orientalism, and to condemn all of it on the basis of a limited selective assessment of a few who worked chiefly on Arab or Islamic Asia. This unfortunate is what Edward Said has done in his extremely influential and, I concede, critically original writings on Orientalism. Orientalism today has become a pejorative term.

One comes across terms such as 'post-Orientalist' in academic pronouncements today (e.g. *Social Science Research Council of U.S.A.*, Annual Report 1991, p.32). Disavowing Orientalism is modish among Western scholars (e.g. the world Orientalist Conference, known as such since the 1980's, has changed its nomenclature to drop the term 'Orientalist'). But the lineaments of the so-called post-orientalist approach are far from being clear. And it will be indeed ironical if our critique of European Orientalists merely mimics present Western critique of its past historiographic practice, if we accept that critique just because that is currently fashionable in Western academic circles. What is the Asian response to European Orientalism? Where is the Asian counter-critique to the Western re-evaluation of previous generation of Western Orientalists?

Were some Eurocentric biases inherent in the Western Orientalists' approach to India and Sinic cultures in the generations from William Jones to Giusepee Tucci? These are the issues which will engage Indologists and ancient history specialists at our Conference. That will be one of the basic questions behind our evaluation of Tucci's own work, from his first paper published in 1911 till his death in 1984—the impressive corpus of his research on Nepal, Tibet, China and India; on Mahayānā Buddhism, Taoism, Confucianism; on Ramakrishna, Aurobindo, Gandhi; on the archaeology of Swat, Southern Tibet, Tantric temples of Nepal; on Asvaghosa, Nāgārjuna and Dinnāga.

The other aspect of great interest to us is the experience he had vis-a-vis Tagore and his institution. As I said earlier, this was an institution conceived as a place for a cultural encounter between the East and West and in this context what was Tucci's experience? It is to this aspect I turn now and, I should like to look into the details a little out of my personal interest in the question, what helps and hinders the growth of the institution? For the present I have depended mainly on the unpublished correspondence between Tucci and Tagore preserved in the Rabindra Bhavana archives; if there are other manuscripts in Tucci's personal papers, I hope that those will become available.

Tucci's regard for Tagore was extraordinary. The earliest surviving letter from Tucci to Tagore speaks of this. This is a letter (printed by Tucci in the form of a birthday greeting card) on 8 May 1926 : " I feel very troubled today because I realize that I cannot express what I have in my heart.... To have the soul of a poet and yet to lack the gift of poetry, it is really a tragic destiny.... Today, Gurudev, I would be a poet like yourself, in order to express to you what I feel. But I myself do not know what I experience in my heart towards you; no word can say it better than *bhakti*; it has in fact the ineffable expressiveness of the undefined." (Tucci to Tagore, 8 May 1926, R.B. Archives, no. 407). This longish letter is full of sentiments of this kind and suggests that Tucci was totally under the spell, so to speak, of the Poet.

When this letter was written Tucci's acquaintance with Tagore was several months old. Tucci had arrived in Santiniketan in November 1925. His compatriot Carlo Formichi spent a shorter time at Santiniketan (he left in March 1926) while Tucci stayed on. It was Formichi who carried the well known letter (21 October 1925) from Mussolini conveying good wishes to Visva-Bharati and a gift of books "with the wish that this offering may always render more and more intense the cultural relations between Italy and the classic land of India, the cradle of the civilization of the world." The visit of Tucci and Formichi was, of course, funded by the Italian government but, in the correspondence between Tucci and Tagore, I have seen no evidence that Tucci was a go-between or mediator between Tagore and Mussolini. On the contrary Tucci was in India when the crucial moment came when Tagore was received by Mussolini in Italy; at that time Formichi's ubiquitous presence was marked, while Tucci was away in Bengal studying Vaishnava literature. In a letter that is undated (but from internal evidence appears to have been written around June 1926) Tucci writes: "Formichi has already written to me that your visit to Italy has been a triumph; I was sure of it. No where perhaps in Europe you are living more than in the heart of my people. But I am very anxious to know the details of your visit to my country; when my wife will come, I shall hear from her.... I am working on my book on the origin of Indian logic, and I am going through the mediaeval Vaisnava literature of Bengal. I have almost finished the *Chaitanya Caritamrita* and I have begun the *Ujjvalnilmani*.... I shall try my best to introduce this literature to our western scholars." (Tucci to Tagore, n.d., cica June 1926). This is an unlikely person at an unlikely place to be Mussolini's agent. In this letter there is a reference to the songs of Natir Pūjā which helps us to date the letter; this play was staged in Santiniketan on May 9, 1926 (vide Ananda Bazar Patrika, 12 May, 1926) and Tagore's visit to Italy commenced on May 30, 1926, with his arrival at Naples. This letter could not be written before the 9th of May, and was possibly written after Tagore left Italy i.e. 22 June1926.

Till this time, i.e. between November 1925 and June 1926, Tucci and his Gurudeva were on the best of terms. Tucci was part of the group accompanying Tagore in February 1926 during his visit to Dacca. (Prabhat Kumar Mukhopadhyay *Rabindra Jibani,* Calcutta 1952, Vol. III, p. 174). Tucci visited eastern Bengal a number of times after that. In December 1926 Tucci writes from Dacca a very interesting letter marking a break. Tagore was abroad from June 1926 to December 1926. He arrived in Santiniketan on 18 December and Tucci writes a few days later. "Gurudev, coming back from Europe you will have been rather astonished seeing that I had left Santiniketan for good. But you know that this is no fault of mine, if some hopeless misunderstanding compelled me to transfer myself somewhere else." Tucci proceeded to say that although he had come to Santiniketan "full of enthusiasm" and had written "some admirative [sic] articles" on that institution, he had changed his views in the recent past; "if I am again asked to write about it I think I shall express myself in a quite different way." What accounted for this change in his approach?

Before we come to that let us note that Tucci takes pains to make two points. First, that he is not motivated by personal grievance. Second, he has not had an opportunity to talk to Tagore frankly about many things he personally observed in Santiniketan. The second point seems to have mattered to Tucci a great deal. "I do not like that you or others may suppose that till I was in Santiniketan, I kept myself silent and when I went away I began my criticism. You know perhaps my sincerity and therefore I hope that you will not have such a bad opinion of my character...." (Tucci to Tagore, 29.12.1926).

What was it which caused a certain disenchantment with Santiniketan, though his personal regard for 'Gurudeva' remained unimpaired? First Tucci, felt that there were many at Santiniketan unworthy of the task of giving shape to Tagore's ideals. "Speaking of your school you said recently that a poet is like a butterfly and those who have to carry into practice his ideals are like silkworms. I wanted specially to entertain [sic] you about those silkworms and the defectiveness of their work because it seems to me that being unable to understand your ideals they are chiefly responsible if the reality of things is not quite in accordance with all that you had in your mind. The consequence is that there is something in the atmosphere of Santiniketan which does not agree with your main idea, to make of it a meeting place of the East and the West". (*ibid*, pp. 2-3). Tucci had kind words about Bidhusekhar Sastri and Kshitimohan Sen, but, of many who remained unnamed, this was his judgement.

The other important point to note in this remarkable letter is the assertion of the value of criticism. Not only does he say that "I did not avoid to say frankly what I felt and certainly not out of a spirit of mere criticism", but also that "progress comes from criticism of friends", (*ibid*, p.2). Further: "because Santiniketan as an international institution belongs to the world, and not to India only, or to a small group of men, and therefore [sic] all those who have some connection with it or are inspired by the same ideals are morally compelled to say what they think about it." (*ibid*).

Tagore's response to this critique of his institution was in studied calm. "I am fully conscious that my own ideals find many obstacles in their realization in my *ashram*, but the same thing would have happened in other parts of the world where the great multitude of men has faith in results that have the stamp of orthodox sanction and therefore are easy and useful. I have seen new educational experiments attempted in several institutions in Europe with big funds and efficient organization, struggling with the same moral difficulties as ours which are inherent in the materials they must use and surroundings that they cannot alter." (Tagore to Tucci, 31 December, 1926, srl. no. 407, p.1).

As for Tucci's personal reactions, Tagore apprehended that "unfavourable impression" was created in his guest's mind by "the scurrilous calumny repeatedly whispered to you behind our back against some of our important members who, at that moment, had no opportunity to defend themselves. However, this has been the usual fate of those who in service of their cause not only trust their own ideals but also all sorts of men who are allowed to come close to their bosom upon which they can easily inflict cruel hurts." (*ibid*, p.1-2). For Tucci, Tagore's affection remained as it was: "nothing has happened which could permanently alienate you from me. Though I was given to understand , when I was in Europe, that your attitude towards our *ashram* had become contemptuously hostile, I never allowed this fact to modify in the least my feelings for you as a friend, and my admiration for you as a very richly gifted scholar." (*ibid*, p.1).

Tucci, in an undated letter to Tagore, fully reciprocated these sentiments about their unimpaired personal relationship. This explanatory letter was written from Dacca, possibly in reply to Tagore's letter of 31 December 1926: "my criticism is the only effect [only the effect] of my love for the institution and not of any personal grievance. Moreover, I changed my opinion not because somebody whispered some calumny to my hear [ear] but only because I myself have seen and noted many details which compelled me to judge rather severely some of those men who are connected with the institution, and I had sufficient arguments to know the moral character of some of them, just on the eve of your departure from Europe." (Tucci to Tagore, n.d. circa January 1927). He went on to express his apprehension about "all what was said to you about me". This was the last letter, among those preserved in our archives, from Tucci to Tagore.

What is striking is the ability of both Tagore and Tucci to rise above differences of opinion and tacit or open criticisms, to preserve mutual affection and regard at the personal level. Tucci was to travel over a vast area from Turkey to Bengal and to visit India nine times; he came to know many leading Indians like Malaviya, Radhakrishnan, Jawaharlal Nehru, Sarojini Naidu et. al.; but Santiniketan, his first introduction to India, remained fresh in his memory and to the end he paid his tribute of love and regard to Tagore. (Interview with A.N. Dar, *Indian Express*, Madras, 13 April 1984). One recalls E.M. Forster's famous words : "Only Connect". Had their been more scholars of the first rank with sincere devotion like Tucci, Santiniketan would have been served better. And yet did the institution have the ability to utilise all the creative and scholarly minds who were attracted by the idea of Visva-Bharati? Tucci's experience was not unique - it was replicated several times with others. (In the collection on Tucci in our archives there is the copy of a letter from Tagore to an unknown person, possibly not Tucci but Sylvain Levi, dated 16 November, 1927. It is of the pattern of Tagore's letter to Tucci of 31.12.1926, cited earlier, full of regrets that the "bond of comradeship" in active association at Santiniketan could not last).

Tagore himself was amply aware of the gaps between his ideals and the institution that developed in Santiniketan, the gap which Tucci pointed at. Repeatedly Tagore chastised himself and his people on this score. "It is a matter of regret that the intellectual ground in Bengal is infertile, unfavourable to make an institution lasting. The infliction of causeless malice from warped minds demolishes what has been created, hurts the sense of purpose, accepts nothing with due respect." (Rachanavali/Sulabh, Vol.XIV, p.281). That was in 1932, a decade after the foundation of Visva-Bharati. Even earlier, in 1925: "Nothing is easier than to ridicule a great ideal. Even the smallest creature can distort something great, and throw dust on it". (*ibid* vol. VII, p.713). And again in one of his last speeches at Santiniketan, about a year before his death : "I do not see anywhere around an endeavour to take up and carry forward with strong resolve that ideal which I started with at this place, that which falters in my days of waning energy and ability." (*ibid* vol. XIV. p. 290). Rabindranath was fully aware of the limits of his endeavour at the institutional level. And yet he was also aware that Institutions generally do not measure up to the lofty ideals, that many others had faced his "difficulties" which were "inherent in the material they must use and surroundings that they cannot alter." (Tagore to Tucci, 31 December, 1926). Thus Tagore in his more pragmatic moment. An Institution may not quite match its ideals. Nevertheless, the Idea provides a goal the Institution should strive towards. This remains a message to us, across the intervening decades, from our Founder Acharya.

Giuseppe Tucci:
A Centenary Obit

2

B. N. Mukherjee

Giuseppe Tucci is an inspiring name in the East-West understanding. Like the Trivikrama (Vishnu) he strode in three steps the three worlds - of course his worlds having been the West, the East and the Future (connecting the first two). The "futurist" historian realised that the survival of the world lay in the synthesis, and not in the contrast, between the East and the West.

Tucci was born on June 5, 1894 at Macerata. As a student he was interested in history, archaeology, sociology, philosophy and language. He learnt Sanskrit from Prof. C. Formici of the University of Rome. He became proficient also in Greek and Latin and acquired some knowledge of Old Persian. Later he studied Chinese and Tibetan.

The academic in Tucci was dissapointed at the stereotyped curricula followed at the University of Rome. However, the scholar in Tucci became active quite early in his life. His article on some Italian inscriptions was published in 1911 (in the *Romische Abteilung* vol. XXVI), when he was just seventeen years old. Soon he was attracted to Indian Philosophy and Buddhism. In 1922 he dealt with the *Karpūramaüjari* of

Rajasekhara. In 1923 he wrote an article on a Buddhist text. The Occidentalist gradually turned into an Indianist.

1925 was a memorable years. Young Tucci arrived at Santiniketan (Bengal, India) to teach Italian, Chinese and Tibetan at the institute founded by Gurudev Rabindra Nath Tagore. To Tucci, Tagore and Gandhi were "two clear and unmistakable voices of the spiritual renewal which was then taking place in India". "Visva-Bharati was the India which gave its hand to Europe, not to the Europe which wished to dominate Asia, but to the Europe which had lived at India's side (undergoing) the same spiritual and intellectual adventures". (*East and West,* 1961, vol. XII, p.111 and 116).

Tucci caught the hands of Visva-Bharati to know how to walk the Indian way. He made friends and began to learn Bengali. Unfortunately, being misunderstood and mentally hurt by some of the so-called well-wishers of the Visva-Bharati he left "the abode of peace"(Santiniketan) with a heavy heart in late 1926. He, however, did not leave India; the Indian wisdom had already begun to unravel itself to him; he had become a profound scholar when he left India (to come back again and again) in 1931.

By that time Tucci had learnt enough Buddhalogy and Tibetology to edit and publish the *Madhyānta-vibhāga-sūtra-bhāshya-ṭīkā* of Sthiramati (jointly with Bidhusekhar Sastri) (1932) and a book in Italian on the Stūpa: Art, Architecture and Symbolism (1932), which became the first volume of his famous Indo-Tibetica series.

Meanwhile, in 1931, he joined the *Instituto Universitario Orientale* of Naples. He taught religion and philosopy at the University of Rome for three decades before retiring in 1969. All through these years he was also very much present in South Asia. He led eight expeditions to Tibet between 1929 and 1948. He explored western and central Tibet, collected enormous number of documents and gained first hand information about Buddhism and the Buddhist way of life in Tibet.

Tucci's interest was extended to Nepal. He led six expeditions to that country (in the period from 1950 to 1954). The knowledge gathered about Nepal helped him to throw new light on dark corners of its history.

By this time the base of all of his operations had become the Instituto Italiano per il Medio ed Estremo Oriente, better known as ISMEO. Tucci founded the Instituto in 1933 and acted its President from 1944 to 1978. Later he became its Honorary President. Assisted by his colleagues at the Institute, Tucci extended the areas of his explorations and enquiries. Investigations of the ISMEO teams at the Swat Valley in Pakistan and also in Afghanistan and Iran led to starting results.

Tucci gradually built up ISMEO into centre of learning of the highest order. The last decades of his life revolved around the Institute. The Great Guru of the present generation of Italian Orientalists passed away on April 5, 1984.

Tucci, the globe trotting scholar, received awards and honours from different bodies in Japan, Thailand, Indonesia, Nepal, India, Pakistan, Afghanistan, Iran, Italy, France, Switzerland, U.K. and Argentina. In Italy he was closely associated with the Academia di Italia. The Jawaharlal Nehru Award for International Understanding has perhaps never been given to a better scholar, who by his work, learning and travelling rendered more service than Tucci to that noble cause.

Nevertheless, Tucci, the scholar, was taller than Tucci, the peace maker. From 1911 to 1983 he published numerous research articles (more than 330 in number) and books (more than 30 in number) on different facets of history and culture, mainly concering Indology (including Tibetan and Nepalese studies). Many of his monographs are signal contributions to our knowledge.

In the *Indo-Tibetica series* (vol.I) the architecture of mchod rten ("a receptacle of offering") and tsha-tsha (*sat-chhaya*; "sachaya,"perfect reproduction") and symbolic meaning of each part of the stūpa were described on the basis of Tibetan texts (like the *Vaidurya-dhar-pa*,etc.) and actual remains. The Temples of Western Tibet (Tsaparang), their sculptures, murals and symbolic meanings were studied in depth in the *Indo-Tibetica*, vol. III. Gyantse and its Monasteries were discussed in the next volume. Seven volumes of this series were published from 1932 to 1941.

The climax of this type of art study was reached with the publication of the *Tibetan Painted Scrolls* (1949). Presented in three volumes, this study deals with the history of Tibet (13-18 century), religious literature, historical literature, biographies and eulogies and discusses in details the evolution of the character of Tibetan *tankas (tan-ko*, "something rolled", Indian *Patas*). Tucci indicated their Indian origin. Unlike many Tibetologists, he was on the firm ground of archaeology and did not depend only on literary texts.

Tucci tried to demonstrate that while the religious architecture, sculptures and icons of Tibet reveal influence from Indian, especially from Kashmir, the civil architecture and craftsmanship were of local origin, though betraying the Chinese impact. One may largely agree with Tucci on these issues; excepting perhaps pointing out that there were also contacts of Tibet with Bengal of the Pāla-Sena age.

In his study of Tantric imagery of Nepal Tucci classified different types of erotic sculptures and explained their significance. To him the union of a male and female deity represents the "loftiest aspiration towards salvation and to the cathersis through which release could be achieved" (*Ratilīlā*, 1969, p.163). In his understanding of Indian sculpture Tucci accepted the androgynous figures as the symbols of the goal that an enlightened man would reach at the end of his long journey. The goal is his integration with the indifferentiated one and the recovery of the synthesis of the opposites" (*Introduction to the Indian Sculpture* by M.Singh).

Tucci, the explorer and archaeologist, was a great admirer of Marco Polo and Sir Marc Aurel Stein. The latters[2] writings often guided his line of investigation. Of the significant discoveries of Tucci during his expeditions were the information acquired from inscriptions, chronicles and tradition about the Khasa rulers of Tibet (and western Nepal) *(Preliminary Reports on Two Scientific Expeditions in Nepal,* 1956) and the Mallas of Nepal *(Nepal, The Discovery of the Mallas,* Italian edition, 1960, and English translation, 1962). We can also include in this list the tombs of Tibetan Kings, including that of Srong-btsen-sgam-po (d.A.D. 649) at Yarlung *(The Tombs of the Tibetan Kings, 1950; The Ancient Civilization of Transhimalaya, 1973)*. The ISMEO team unearthed in the Swat Valley (Pakistan) prehistoric antiquities (including items of Gandhār grave culture) and historic monuments and sculptures (of the Buddhist affiliation).

To Tucci we owe critical editions and studies of several important texts. We have already referred to his effort in this direction jointly with Bidhusekhar Sastri. We can here especially refer to his edition and studies of the Karpūramānjari of Rajasekhara (1922), *Abhisamayalamkaraloka* of Haribhadra (1932), *Trisatikayah Prajnaparamitayah karikasaptatih* of Asanga (a commentary on the *Vajrachhedika,* discovered by Tucci himself) (*Minor Buddhist Texts,* I, 1956).

Tucci's several articles on ancient texts indicate his love for literature. He made a collection of folk songs of Tibet from the direct of Gyantse. He followed, in this case, the lead already given by S.C.Das, O'conner, van Mannen, Franke, Roerich and Bell.

On the basis of the old Tibetan texts (including the *Blue Annals*) Tucci reconstructed (in 1933) the biography of Rin-

Chen-bzan-po (born in 958), a senior contemporary of Atisa. He helped in the revival of Buddhism in Tibet. He was also a great translator. He is considered to have introduced Buddhist logic in Tibet.

In five lectures delivered at the University of Calcutta, Tucci established that Maitreya (nātha), the supposed author of the *Abhisamayalankara karika, Madhyantavibhaga, Mahayana-sutralankara*, etc., was a historical person, who contributed to the Yogachara doctrine. (*On Some Aspects of the Doctrines of Maitreya (natha) and Asanga*,1930,)

Though primarily interested in Buddhism and early history, Tucci was very much aware of the modern Indian developments, especially in the field of religious movements. In 1936 he paid his tribute to Ramakrishna Paramahansa. Two other modern Indians who charmed Tucci were, as noted above, Gurudev Rabindra Nath and Mahatma Gandhi.

Tucci's ideas about philosophy were expressed in various writings. His magnum opus in this regard was *Storia della Filosofia indiana*, published in 1957.

Tucci, the explorer, was naturally interested in historical geography. He wrote about the travels of Tibetan pilgrims in the Swat Valley. His team followed the path of Alexander in choosing the sites of excavation in the same region in the sixth decade of this century.

The great scholar did not live in an ivory tower, cut-off from the general public. He wrote several monographs in Italian to disseminate among educated public the knowledge about Tibet and several other areas and subjects. *The Ancient Civilization of Transhimalaya,* which is an English translation of his Tibet, both published in 1993, presents in a popular style the archaeological materials on Tibet, emphasising for the first time on the prehistoric implements of the region. This monograph is a major work to popularise ancient knowledge.

Tucci was a great organiser and academic administrator. The ISMEO was founded by him in 1933 for developing Oriental studies without being bogged down in the swamps of the university curricula. Efforts were made to collect various types of source materials. It has an excellent library and an efficient excavation unit (which worked in Pakistan, Afghanistan, Iran, etc.). It set up a museum in the Swat area and arranged the antiquities in museums in Kabul and Ghazani. Tucci and his students and colleagues worked indeed as Italy's cultural envoys to the Orient.

Tucci, unlike many Orientalists and scholars of Western civilization, believed in the historical unity of Eurasia. In the fifties he was of the opinion that Italy, with no hang-over of colonial rule in Asia in modern times and with a history of contacts with Asia in early times, was ideally suited to "find points of contact, not contrast, (and) of synthesis between the cultures of the West and the East". He was a humanist as well as an Orientalist.

This humanistic attitude and the unfailing belief in the intrinsic value of man led him to travel and mix with people all over the world. The seer in Tucci realised that "under every sky man has the some dreams; he is the same creature, painfully suspended between the heaven and earth; fearfully alone befor the mystery of life and death".

The contributions of Tucci to Oriental studies, particularly to the history of Buddhism, Tibet and Nepal are enormous. His researches in the historicity of Maitreyanātha, non-religious history, archaeology and art of Tibet and political history of Nepal will be eternally recognised in the world of Oriental studies. Tucci was at once an explorer, an archaeologist, a historian, an art-critic and a linguist all rolled into one. A humanist and a pacifist, he studies history, laying stress on the ultimate unity of the fundamental culture of man, his hero.

Though one of the greatest even Orientalists, he was comparatively unknown to Indian scholars, at least up to the sixth decade of this century. One of the reasons was that his early major publications were mostly in Italian. Even the volumes of the great Indo-Tibetica series were originally published (1932-1947) in Italian. These were translated into English only in later years of the last decade. However, at the time of his demise he was a world figure, a colossus standing with his feet spanning the distance between the East to the West.

Long ago, in 1925, a shy young man came to Santiniketan, "the abode of peace", in search of knowledge and peace. He came to an institution already hallowed by the presence of great teachers, including some Europeans. But the restless soul of the bird could not rest at a place where the world had been hoped to become "a single nest". Edged out of the nest, he had to fly in the open sky over the globe, but hovering again and again in the Indian atmosphere. He soared higher and higher reaching ultimately eternity, leaving behind the chirping music of universal brother-hood and scholarship.

Professor Giuseppe Tucci: The Man

3

Ram Singh Tomar

Professor Giuseppe Tucci was a student of Professor Carlo Formichi at the University of Rome. Professor Formichi was a student of Michele Kerbakar. Kerbakar was a great Sanskritist. Italy was perhaps the first European country where a complete translation of two great Indian epics into Italian was done. The *Vālmiki Rāmāyaṇa* was translated in full from the original Sanskṛit by Gaspare Gorressio and the *Mahābhārata* by Michele Kerbakar. A copy of the Italian translation of the *Rāmāyaṇa* by Gorressio was available in the personal collection of Boro *dada* - elder brother of Gurudeva - Dwijendra Nath Thakur as informed by Formichi in his book '*India and Indians*'. Boro *dada* had asked Formichi to translate into English preface of Gorressio.

Professor Carlo Formichi, Professor of Sanskrit at the University of Rome knew intimately Kalidas Nag. Professor Nag promised Formichi that on his behalf he will request Rabindranath Tagore to pay a visit to Italy on a lecture tour. A friend of Formichi, advocate D.J. Irani of Bombay also promised him to request and persuade the Poet to pay a visit to Italy. Dr. Nag wrote to Formichi that the Poet has been invited by the Government of Argentina in December 1924 to participate in the Century Celebrations of the Republic of that Nation and en route to Argentina he along with his secretary, Dr. Nag and two professors of his university will take a ship from Spain. The Government of Spain had also invited the Poet to deliver a course of lectures which the Poet had accepted. Rathindranath was at that moment in London, and he informed Formichi that his father will leave Buenos Aires for Geneva on 2nd January 1925. The Poet's health was somewhat delicate and a very flexible programme was chalked out by Formichi and his Italian friends. The Poet learnt from Formichi about the political condition prevailing in Italy. He was accorded a very cordial welcome with great ovation on 19th January 1925 at the fort of Geneva. Though the Poet was on a private visit, but the news of his arrival spread in Geneva as a news of the day. The authorities of the city, young people, correspondents flocked around the world famous great poet of the Orient; citizens of Geneva formed lines on both the sides of the broad avenue to have a glimpse of the eminent personality.

He was escorted by Formichi to Milan. His reception at Milan was triumphant, people from all walks of life and of every political shade-fascists, non-fascists gathered, and he was received by the President of Philological Association of Milan. In the evening the Poet attended the famous Scala Theatre and saw the performance of the opera Trairate of G. Verdi directed by famous director Toscamini. Formichi in his book '*India and Indians*' has given details of the visit to Milan. The Poet was suffering from influenza and was administered medicine. Formichi has reproduced the medical certificate dated 25th January 1925. On account of the illness of the Poet all the engagements, receptions had to be cancelled and curtailed. One day the Poet expressed the idea of inviting Prof. Formichi to come to Santiniketan as professor of Sanskrit for one semester and whether in turn he would collect funds to institute a Chair for Italian language and literature and arrange for a gift of suitable books to let young Indian students get a knowledge of Italian literature and arts. Formichi became very happy at this noble proposal of establishing cultural exchange with India. But for want of means it remained unfulfilled.

The Poet embarked on 2nd February 1925 from Venice. He universely liked Venice, the city without noise, dust, smoke and other consequent worries. It was beautiful and a joy for ever. On 20th August 1925 the Poet sent a telegram to Professor Formichi from Calcutta inviting him as a visiting professor for the period from November to March on the same terms as for previous visiting professors. Official letter of the governing committee was to follow shortly. 'After about twenty days he got a letter from Kalidas Nag saying that in reciprocation the Poet was hoping to have the services of a professor to teach Italian and a gift of suitable books on Italian art, aesthetics, and literature in addition to some books sent by Dr. Tucci. Formichi approached the Ministry of Public Instruction and Foreign Affairs but did not get any encouraging response. Finally he wrote to the Head of the Stae H.E. Mussolini. Summary in English of the letter is reproduced here.

Excellency, the University of Visva-Bharati after having invited during the past years European Indologists Sylvian Levi from Paris, Mourice Winternitz from Prague, and Sten Konow from Christiana for imparting a course in Sanskrit has now approached me as a representative of the Italian Indology. This is an honour to the Italian scholarship. The authorities have sanctioned me leave. Before leaving for India I am approaching your Excellency not to these empty handed.... European professors who preceded me were granted by their respective governments gift of books. I would also like to carry with me a good gift of books. I am enclosing a list of books. It would also be in fitness of things if an Italian scholar capable of teaching Italian culture is sent.

Expenses of my travel and maintenance in India will be met by the Visva-Bharati but the cost of travel and maintenance of the second scholar be kindly be provided by Italy.

The new champion of the new school of Italian Indianists was Dr. Giuseppe Tucci, Deputy Librarian in the library of Parliament and Reader-in-charge of Religion and Philosophy of India and the Far East in the University of Rome, who had a profound knowledge of Oriental Languages and at the same time eminently suitable to enhance the prestige of Italian scholarsip.

I shall be very happy to present personally the gift of your Excellency to the poet of world fame. My departure has been fixed for 4th November from Brindis.

With profound regards I remain, your Excellency's most devoted Carlo Formichi. His Excellency Mussolini not only sanctioned in donation the books listed by me but added many more and assigned the job of Teaching Italian at Visva-Bharati to Tucci. An English translation of the letter of Mussolini is as follows.

Rome, 21 October 1925, 'Illustrious Professor',

An expressing very heartly pleasure for the invitation extended to you by the university of Visva-Bharati, which honours the Italian scholar and Italian scholarship and the gift in my name to the university, the best centre of Indian culture. The books listed are enclosed with the best wishes that the gift will help in establishing cultural relations between Indian cradle of civilisation of the world and Italy. Believe my Illustrious Professor Mussolini.

Formichi arrived in Santiniketan, the Poet welcomed the guest in a beautiful ceremony. Pandit Vidhushekhar Bhattacharya read a welcome address in Sanskrit and Formichi replied by delivering a touching address, which deserves to be published in translation. His concluding words were: "The

Prime Minister himself desired that I (Formichi) along with a magnificient collection of books should express also his special pleasure in initiating cultural exchange between India and Italy. I am, therefore, proud to be able to offer for this fraternity of scholars the gift of Benito Mussolini and to represent not only the intimate friendly sentiments of my people and also the consent of the Great Men who Govern the destinay of my Motherland". The daily routine of the two Italian Professors was to take classes and in the afternoon from four to five they were often invited by the Poet for tea, generally at times he was alone or at times in the company of other visiters. Formichi in his book '*India & Indians*' has given details in a fascinating manner. After that the professor used to go on a brisk stroll with Tucci. What Formichi thought about Tucci I give a translation of the passage in Italian.

Tucci seen afterwards joined me in abode of peace to teach Italian language and literature to enhance the prestige of Italy and his government.

Giuseppe Tucci who did me the honour to have him as my student is without doubt a man of exception. He has just entered by thirtieth year his knowledge is already wonderful. Besides Sanskrit and several Indian literary details he knows Chinese and Tibetan. He is familiar with Iranian and languages of Central Asia which have been discovered just a few years back. He is specially gifted in learning language. He has a passion to know to do research and to understand thoroughly and that compels him to spend day and night amongst the books, manuscripts, maps and ruins. He is like a voluntary martyr and in the depth of that man one finds sweetness, the very reason of his existence.

At Santiniketan Tucci with his life of scholarship, with immensity of his linguistic knowledge and prompt readiness of his comprehension impressed everybody in general and admiration brought him close to the Poet, who in him recognised the future prince of the Orientalists.

"I love him like my son, I found in him a friend in my daily strolls and exercises."

In February 1925 the Poet was invited by the University of Dacca to deliver lectures and he asked Formichi and Tucci to accompany him. In Dacca Formichi delivered three lectures and from there they went to Mymensingh. They were guests of the Maharaja, Formichi delivered lecture on the Atharvaveda in Anand Mohon College. Both before going to Dacca and on their return were guests of the Poet in Jorasank. The Poet fell ill and Pandit Vidushekhar Bhattacharya gave a hearty send-off in the traditional manner. The ceremony was touching. Students and members of staff bade farewell. Formichi left Santiniketan on 4 March 1925 for Banaras and returned to Calcutta on 11th March and left for Bombay to sail for Italy. Tucci accompanied him all the way. He did not want to leave him alone till he left India. Before leaving for Bombay Gurudeva arranged solemn ceremony and thanked Formichi for his cooperation and wished him a happy journey and gave a massage for Italian people. "Among other things, the Poet remarked, About the cultural bonds that your coming to Santiniketan and presenting a collection of books I must mention your former disciple Dr. Tucci, who remains with us and for lending his series I cannot thank your government in sufficient measure. He has studied with wonderful comprehension. His knowledge of ancient culture of India is amazing; he has followed the triumphant history of Buddhism in remote regions.... These sentiments the Poet reiterated in a letter written afterwards. Gurudev gave many presents and ten volumes of his works.

The Poet was invited by Benito Mussolini to visit Italy as a guest of the Government of Italy. He with his retinue reached Italy on 30 May 1926. Formichi received him on behalf of Mussolini. Account of his visit has been extensively published by several Indians scholars. While Gurudeva was in Italy, Tucci left Santiniketan for good. The reason for his bidding a farewell to the *ashram* where he had came to stay for long and he was as affectionate to the Master better be understood by referring to the exchange of letters between the two. A bit earlier on May 8, 1926, on the birthday of Gurudev, Tucci published a small booklet expressing his heart felt felicitations: "I feel very touched today because I realize that I cannot express what I have in my heart.... I am a scholar, Gurudev, and sometimes scholarship to poetry...."

Let the small me send their good wishes to small men, but to you! And what can we wish to you! Nothing. Because the wings of your poetry and the message of love that you have sung to the world have carried you beyond the boundaries of time.... No wishes therefore, but rather thanks-giving and prayer; thanks giving for what you have already given to us, prayer for what you must still give us.

Giuseppe Tucci

I quote from a letter dated 29.12.1926.

'Gurudev, coming back from Europe, you will be rather astonished seeing that I had left Santiniketan for good. But you know that this is no fault of mine, if some hopeless misunderstanding compelled me to transfer myself somewhere else. I regret very much to have been deprived of the company of as good and learned friends as Shastri and Sen are, and to have lost the opportunity I had there to learn from you so many things, as I did in our daily meetings'....

Giuseppe Tucci stayed in India for more than five years teaching at Dacca and Calcutta universities. He mastered Bengali language and made many eminent scholars his friends. He corresponded with Gurudev and he in turn wrote very appreciative and affectionate letters to Tucci. The misunderstanding was cleared, which was created by some petty persons who wrote scurrilous letters in an attempt at character assassination, and which had hurt Tucci and also Rabindranath Tagore when he learnt about it. Gurudeva lost a brilliant scholar and Tucci lost the opportunity to enjoy the company of a great world-famed personality. But Tucci's admirtion for Gurudeva and his ideals never diminished in his whole life. He said in his memoirs that his stay in India for five years changed his mental horizon and whole outlook. He studied thoroughly mediaeval Bengali literature and remarked that after the classical Indian literature the mediaeval Bhakti literature was next great literary event in Indian culture.

In 1948 in the Senate Hall of the University of Allahabad I had a rare privilege to listen a very learned lecture delivered by Professor Giuseppe Tucci on Tibetan Religious Art. He had returned from his academic exploration of Tibet and he had brought with him a large number of Tibetan painted banners, known as *Tankas*. The lecture was highly acclaimed and the Chairman Professor Iswari Prasad praised him in very eloquent words. I had not even imagined that in future I shall have the privilege to work under his guidance and with him.

In 1950 I was selected by the University of Ercating to go to Italy and work in the ISMEO and Rome University. Professor Tucci was Presiednt of the ISMEO. I arrived there on the Christmas day. The city bore a festive look. After the vacations for Natale (Christmas) were over, I was taken to Professor Tucci's chamber in a big room; well decorated by artistic furniture and pictures on the walls. I had taken with me two introductory letters from Professor P.L. Vaidya - then Mayurbanj Professor of Sanskrit at the Hindu University, Banaras and Professor Probodh Chandra Bagchi. Both of them had a great admiration for Tucci and had told me that he was a scholar who always inspired young scholars and both of them, while studying in Paris had visited Tucci. Tucci took these letters and said "oh! you known them, how are they?" He was very prompt in correspondence. Before my letters informing Professor Vaidya and Bagchi about my safe arrival in Rome reached them, they wrote that Professor Tucci had already written to them in reply to their letters.

A few days later Prof. Tucci invited me at his residence in Rome, Vescore Squar No.21. It was a big house on the first floor. His personal library was impressing with volumes well arranged in the wooden shelves. On the door in glittering bold brass letters in Devanagari script was inscribed the summum bonum of the central theme of the Mahayani Buddhists:

Ye dharma hetuprabhava hetu tesham tathagato hiavadayat
Tesham ca yo nirodha evam vadi mahasramanah//

Northern Buddhism technicaly known as the Mahayana was a favourite subject of study of Prof. Tucci. In the contemporary Buddhist scholars none knew better than him Tibet and its environs. Many of his co-nationals took him to be a Buddhist. He believed in the tenets of Buddhism. His house was full of Tibetan ritualistic objects. Tibetan of religious temperament always chanted *Om mani Padma hum* and the Japanese monks Namyo Hore Gye Kyam (obesience) to the lotus of perfect religion *Saddharma Pundariksha*. He had given his only son the name Ananda. He had a lure for the mountains and also wanted to discover and to know intimately the northern Buddhism. He made eight academic expeditions in Tibet- all the expenditions were meticulously organised, with a team of doctor, photographers, cooks and porters. In one of these the legendary mountaineer Tenzing accompanied him. He travelled in those difficult lands on foot. Once his caravan was camping at a height of 15000 feet and one Alice Getty-Englishman met him. He has written that only a person like Tucci could provide a five course hot meal at that altitude. The results of these expeditions have been published giving information about the rich material of historical, artistic and literary value. He made two expeditions in western Nepal. When entry into Tibet and the Himalayas became impossible, he shifted his archaeological activities to Swat in Pakistan, Afganistan and Eastern Iran. All the important finds are exhibited in the National Museum of Oriental Art of Rome which came into existence at his initiative.

When last year my scholar historian friend Vice-Chancellor of Visva-Bharati informed me that the universiy will organise birth centenary seminar of Professor Tucci in collaboration with the cultural centre of Italian embassy at Delhi I proposed to write a biography of Tucci in Hindi with whom I lived for five years. He welcomed the proposal and provided some financial assistance for its publication. I visited Italy on my own to meet my old colleagues and students and collect some more material about him. I thought it was necessary to visit Italy. While in Rome very often I used to visit Tucci at his residence. On week-ends he used to visit the house of his wife madam Fransesca Bonardi Tucci at San paolo di Cavalieri, a small hill station about 60 kms from Rome. The house is situated on the top of the hill in olive garden. Lady Francesca Bonardi is a very gifted woman, and an excellent photographer. She accompanied Prof. Tucci in the expenditions in Nepal and Swat. In 1970 Tucci left his house at Rome and shifted in San paolo di cavalieri. He donated his excellent library to the ISMEO and kept with him only a few thousand books. We visited Signora Francesca Tucci. She has carefully preserved the archival materials of Tucci. Due to lack of time we could not examine the huge mass of material. She took us to the room where the great orientalist breathed his last. *Ye dharma hetu prabhava* — the Mahavakya of the Mahayanis was glittering as ever; over the study table the autographed portrait of Gurudeva which the Poet presented him in 1926 was still there.

To complete the chronicle Giuseppe Tucci was born in Macerate, provincial Capital of Marche in Central Italy. I visited the town with one Professor Signor Antonio Viglietti. The grateful citizens of Macerate have placed a marble table on the entrance of the house where Tucci was born saying that the famous oriantalist Tucci was born there. He took his degree from the Rome University in 1930 he was appointed university professor of Chinese Language and Literature and in 1932 at Rome University, as Professor of Indian philosophy and Far East. Recently Mussolini papers have been published and as I was short of time I requsted my Italian friends kindly to send me all the references made about India. It is a big task but one important reference has been sent to me saying that Tucci presented H.E. Benito Mussolini to his Excellency Subhash Chandra Bose. Tucci was one of the close academician who could approach the Duce, the Italian Head of the State. He was nominated the honour - Academic of Italy in 1929, while he was still in India.

Orientalists from all over the world frequented him. During my tenure in Rome Prof. S.K. Chatterrjee, Dr. S. Radhakrishnan, Sri R. Vankataraman (former President of India). Dr. N.P. Chakravarty (D.G. of Archaelogical Survey of India), A.S. Altekar, V. Raghavan, Amarnatha Jha (V.C. Allahabad University) and many others visited him. All were accorded a hearty welcome at ISMEO. At his initiative Laurea was conferred on Prof. S.N. DasGupta, Dr. Radhakrishnan and S.K.Chatterji, by Rome University. He was conferred honorary academic titles from many universities and received Nehru Award for International understanding. Intentionally I am omitting the controversy whether Gurudev approved Fascism or was against the system in spite of the fact that he enjoyed the warm hospitality offered as a State guest by the Italian Duce S.E. Benite Mussolini. I shall refer to the articles written by Ramanand Chattopadhyay in modern review of those years and the faithful account given by Prof. Formichi in his book in Italian India and Indians, Milan- 1943.

Tucci remained a strong supporter of the ideals of Rabindranath Tagore. His reverence for the Poet never diminished, a visible proof being the organisation of Birth Centenary Celebrations of the Poet in 1961. The ceremony was organised in the mayoral office of Rome, the most celebrated place in Rome, the Campidogloi (Capital). Professor Humayun Kabir delivered the inaugural speech. A galaxy of scholars, Vice-chancellors of Italian universities, poets and writers attended the function. A special issue of the Quarterly East West was published on the occasion.

In the last years of his life Tucci became a firm believer in the concept that there is only one continent, Eurasia not two Europe and Asia. They have only a few contrasts, and many common traits in culture and thought.

Tagore and Tucci

4

Ujjal Kumar Majumdar

On the way back home from Argentina via Europe in an Italian ship, Rabindranath Tagore got down at Genoa on January 21, 1925. Mussolini had just started clamping down on democratic forces. He tried to camouflage his intentions with a vigorous propaganda drive which an outsider like Rabindranath could not see through. Mussolini arranged for invitations to be sent to him from important cities of Italy. Rabindranath delivered a lecture on music at Milan under the presidentship of Duke Scottle, was given an ovation at the People's Theatre, and wrote a poem on Italy. But he was not feeling well and, after a few days at Venice, left for India on February 2. Carlo Formichi, a renowned Orientalist, served as his interpreter during his short stay.

On November 28, 1925, Formichi came to Santiniketan with a big bundle of Italian books as presents from Mussolini. A young academic named Giuseppe Tucci accompanied him. Rabindranath thought Mussolini was really a well-wisher of India. But soon news came of murders of writers such as Amendola and Mattiotti. Benedetto Croce was not allowed to go out of Naples and Duke Scottie's movements too were restricted, provoking protests from intellectuals of other countries led by Romain Rolland.

At this critical moment Mussolini sent through Formichi, who had returned home on March 19, 1926, an invitation to Rabindranath to visit Italy again. Tucci was then at Santiniketan, teaching Chinese and studying religious texts. To the surprise of every one, Rabindranath accepted the invitation. He knew nothing of the developments in Italy, and it was Formichi and Tucci who tried their best to keep him in the dark on his last visit. This time (in May-June 1926) Rabindranath was given a right royal reception in Rome by Mussolini, in whose presence he spoke on art in theatre hall, and attended a festival of children's songs in the Colliseum. Rabindranath discovered the truth after meeting Croce, who was brought to Rome from Naples at his request and then from Duke Scottie. Then, in June-July, Rolland apprised him of the situation in detail at Villeneuve. In September, Rabindranath wrote an open letter, published in the *Manchester Guardian* and other important European newspapers, severely criticizing Mussolini's atrocities. On returning to Santiniketan in December, he found that Tucci had left. On Decembar 29, he received a rather long letter from Tucci in Dacca University.

Gurudev,

Coming back from Europe you will have been rather astonished seeing that I had left Santiniketan for good. But you know that there is no fault of mine, if some hopeless misunderstanding compelled me to transfer myself somewhere else. I regret very much to have been deprived of the Company of so good and learned friends as Sastri and Sen are, and to have lost the opportunity. I had there to learn from you so many things, as I did in our early meetings. But I have no responsibility for all this. Only I regret my sudden departure did prevent me to speak to you frankly about many things and specially about Santiniketan.

Having come to your place full of enthusiasm and having also written some very adulatory articles on Santiniketan as soon as I went there, I feel myself rather compelled to explain why, if I am again invited to write about it, I think that I shall express myself in an quite different way. I do not like that you or others may suppose that till I was in Santiniketan, I kept myself silent and when I went away I began my criticism. You know perhaps my sincerity and therefore, I hope that you will not have such a bad opinion of my character; moreover, any one of my friends in Santiniketan knows clearly my ideas because I did not avoid to say frankly what I felt and certainly not out of a spirit of mere criticism, but because Santiniketan, as an international institution, belongs to the world and not to India only or a small group of men, and therefore, all those who have some connection with it or are inspired by the same ideas are morally compelled to say what they think about it. Progress comes out from criticism of friends. Moved by this spiritual and intellectual interest I had in my mind to point out to you all what I had oppurtunity to see these in about one year. Speaking of your school you said recently that a poet is like a butterfly and those who have to carry out into practice his ideas are like silkworms. I wanted specially to entertain you about those silkworms and the defectiveness of their work because it seems to me that being unable to understand your ideals they are chiefly responsible if the reality of things is not quite in accordance with all that you had in your mind. The consequence is that there is something in the atmosphere of Santiniketan which does not agree with your main idea, to make of it a meeting place of the East and the West. But of course, I cannot entertain you on those things in a single letter, specially because I cannot come to detail. Moreover, being to general, my criticism could seem the expression rather of a personal grievance, than of a sincere and (*illegible*) love for the institution. I hope that I shall meet you and have a frank talk with you on the eve of my leaving Santiniketan.

I would have liked to receive a complete set of works which now I can understand quite well - not as a recompense for the *(illegible)* that I may have done, but as a mark of love. Nobody realized how such a gift could have been appreciated by me; and I myself did not ask for it remembering that what is asked is in fact bought.

I hope that you are in good health.

Yours truly,
G. Tucci
c/o. Dacca University

This unpublished letter suggests that Tucci had to face some unpleasentness at Santiniketan because of his activities in Italy. Though he blames his departure on some "hopeless misunderstanding" for which he was not responsible, it was he who carried out Mussolini's instructions to insulate Rabindranath from anti-fascist activities during his tour.

That Tucci did substantial work on Indian literature at Santiniketan is evident from another unpublished and undated letter he wrote to Rabindranath in Italy:

Gurudev your photo is beautiful, but your letter is sad. Do not feel homesick. Do try rather to take rest, complete rest and be not too kind towards your admires. Formichi has already written to me that your visit to Italy has been a truimph. I am sure of it. Nowhere perhaps in Europe you are living more than in the heart of my people.

But I am very anxious to know the details of your visit to my country. When my wife will come, I shall hear from her the enthusiasm of Rome. About myself, I have nothing to tell you. I am working on my book on the origin of Indian logic, and I am going through the mediaeval Vaishnava Literature of Bengal. I have almost finished the *Chaitanya Charitamrita* and I have begun the *Ujjvalanilamani*. I think that after Buddhism this is the greatest creation of Indian mind and I shall try my best to introduce this literature to our western scholars. The articles on Natir Puja is almost finished. In order to feel again in my soul the ineffable and deep melody of your songs, I expressed my desire to many to hear somebody singing some of the most beautiful songs of your drama. The sisters of Santosh were kind enough to accept my request and you were with us, Gurudev, while they were singing and the sun was dying behind the many coloured curtain of the rainy clouds.

Great is the distance which separates us, but my heart is always with you. Humbly asking you blessings,

Yours
G. Tucci

In another letter from Santiniketan to Rabindranath, dated October 6, 1926, Tucci gives details of his study of Bengali literature and speaks his mind on his Santiniketan colleagues:

Gurudev,

I am sorry that I could not write to you before. I was for some days on tour in Vikrampur district and then as soon as I came back, I feel ill. Now I feel better, though I cannot say that I am perfectly well.

I thank you very much for kind presents. My Bengali is now quite all right and I can read any kind of books. I read *Goraksa Vijay, Candidas, Vidyapati* etc. Now I am studying *Krishnakirtan*, but I do not find it as attractive as the other poems of Candidas.

I am sorry that my last letter was perhaps not quite clear. My criticism is the only effect of my love for the institution and not of any personal grievances. Moreover I changed my opinion not because somebody whispered some calumnies to my ear but only because I myslf have seen and noted many details which compelled me to judge rather severely some of those men who are connected with the institution and I have sufficient arguments to know the moral characters of some of them. Just on the eve of your departure for Europe, the letter which I received regarding the free passage on the steamer opened my eyes; and I know all what was said to you about me just on that occassion and later on. Of course all this was more than sufficient to make me very careful about my relations with those whom I could not any longer consider to be sincere enough to have any connection with me. But my enthusiasm for the ideal is unchanged and I hope that it will be possible for you to find one day or another somebody who is really coscious of the great responsibility of receiving an (*illegible*) as Santiniketan is.

I shall remain in Dacca till April. Then I will go to the hills for about three months. After summer I hope to go to Benares or to Madras where I wish to stay some months in order to study Dravidian dialects.

I hope you are keeping well.

Yours sincerely
G.Tucci

Amidst all this bitterness Tucci must have found some solace in a letter dated December 31, 1926, which Rabindranath had written in reply to his letter of December 29:

Dear Friend,

I felt very much relieved when I received your letter this morning, for I was assured that nothing has happened which could parmanently alienate you from me. Though I was given to understand when I was in Europe that your attitude towards our *Ashram* had become contemptuously hostile, I never allowed this fact to modify in the least my feelings for you as a friend and my admiration for you as a very richly gifted scholar. I am fully conscious that my own ideals find many obstacles in their realization in my *Ashram*, but the same thing would have happend in other parts of the world where the great multitude of men has faith in results that have the stamp of orthodox sanction and therefore are easy and useful. I have seen educational experiments attempted in several institutions in Europe with big funds and efficient organisation, struggling with the same moral dificulties as ours which are inherent in the materials they must use and surroundings that they cannot alter. But the most unfortunate factor in our case which created the most unfavourable impression in your mind was the scurrilous calumny repeatedly whispered to you behind our back against some of our important members who at that moment had no opportunity to defend themselves. However this has been usual fate of those who in the service of their cause not only trust their own ideas but also all sorts of men who are allowed to come close to their bosom upon which they can easily inflict cruel hurts.

I earnestly hope that we shall have occasion to meet again and in the meanwhile do not forget that I am.

Your affectionate friend,
Rabindranath Tagore

In the end Tucci will be remembered as one of the finest Orientalists in the world. After active service during World War I, he graduated from the University of Rome (1919) and began his Chinese studies, which resulted in volumes such as *Scritto di Mencio* (1921), *Storia della filosofla Cinese antica* (1922) and *Saggezza Cinese* (1926). When he came to India he was working on Indian Philosophy (*Lince di una storia della materialismo Indiano*, two volumes, 1923-1929). Tucci felt that the history of Asia was inter-connected with that of Europe, and that Eurasia should be treated as a single unit in cultural as well as geographical terms.

Tucci knew Sanskrit and Tibetan in depth and had more than working knowledge of Chinese, Pali and some modern Indian languages other than Bengali.

The six years Tucci spent in India were crucial to his carrier, as were eight expeditions to Tibet (1929-48), six to Nepal (1950-1954) and his explorations in Pakistan, Afghanistan and Iran (1955-1959). He conducted archaeological research till 1976, producing some excellent books of general interest, among them *To Lhasa and Beyond* (1956), *The Discovery of the Mallas* (1962), *Tibet: Land of Snow* (1967), and *Rati-Lila* (1969).

Winner of the Jawharlal Nehru Award for International Understanding in 1976, Tucci was the Chairman of the Departmetn of Religion and Philosopy of India and the Far East at the University of Rome from 1932 to 1969. He died on April 5, 1984, in his house at San Paulo dei Cavalieri, near Tivoli.

(Letters quoted by courtesy of Visva-Bharati)

Giuseppe Tucci: As Aesthete

5

Kalpika Mukherjee

In the two volumes out of seven of the Indo Tibetica, Prof. Giuseppe Tucci has given the description of the temples of the Western Tibet built during the 10th century A.D. under the tireless supervision of Rin-Chen-Zan-Po, whose name, Tucci says, "will remain for ever connected to one of the most important periods in the history of Tibetan art". Tucci recovers the invaluable treasures of Tibetan temple art with utmost difficulty from the ruins of the temples, (identifies the temples belonging to the particular deities, along with the *Tantric maṇḍalas*) explains their symbolism and finally gives an analysis and appreciation of the paintings and sculptures as work of art.

Giuseppe Tucci is not only a scholar of extra-ordinary versatility, proficient in the history of Tibet, India and China and Tibetan Tantric literature and religion, he is equally proficient in Hindu and Buddhist art, its manifestation in different countries in different ages. He does not observe the temples of Tibet with the eyes of only a scholar, but the way he makes an assessment of the temple art of Western Tibet and Nepal shows that he is a real connoisseur, a '*sahṛdaya*', in the truest sense of the term, who drinks from the foun-tain of the beauty of the temple paintings where the full maturity of the artistic minds had manifested themselves. The very title of the books viz. *The Temples of Western Tibet and their Artistic Symbolism* is suggestive.

Historically Buddhism entered Western Tibet in 7th century A.D. Hoffman and Franche have elaborately discussed it in their books, *The Religion of Tibet* and the *Antiquity of Indian Tibet* respectively. In this connection the contributions of the great missionary Rin-Chen-Zan-Po and his royal partrons deserve special mention. Buddhism which had been already prevalent there, got a special impetus from the aesthetic presentation of the Tantric rituals which refer to fourfold Tantric practices. viz.,

1. *kriyā tantra* -(bya rgyud): It is based on external practices or formulas, various propitiatory rites, magical liturgies, contemplation on the images of gods, painted mainly on the '*paṭas*', manifestations of various *mudrās* in performing art.

2. *caryā tantra*— (spyed rgyud): Here an equilibrium of external practices, verbal and physical, prevails. The *sādhaka* is expected to observe a pure and proper livelihood with the purity of body, speech and mind.

3. *yoga tantra*—(rnal byor rgyud): It consists of yoga or practice or '*upāya*' joined to gnosis or prajña. It takes place internally in the initiate's heart, in a meditative principle. In this stage mantra is no more the simple recital of the formulas. The mystical meaning of sound, its vibrations and its cosmic co-relations are understood.

4. *advaya tantra*—(gnis med 'pai rgyuḍ): referring to the anuttara yoga (bla na med 'pai rnal byor) in which the duality between the subject and the object is obliterated. It emphasises the identity between practice '*upāya*' and

gnosis, '*prajña*'. It is a re-integration of the Absolute through the experience of duality. Symbolically the 'yuganaddha' icons represent such state of mental sublimity.

The introduction of Tantric iconography and monastery architecture in Tibet are historical events. Tradition affirms that Padmsambhava and Santarkṣita made the 'bsam yas' monastery in Tibet on the model of the odantapurī mahāvihāra of India. At that time there were three *mahāvihāras* or monastic universities in India. These are — *Odantapurī*, *Vikramśīla* and *Nālanda*. 'Bsam yas' was built under the influence of all these, especially of *Odantapuri*. Evidently, however, Indian art and architecture had an uninterrupted entry in the Tibetan monasteries since then.

Art was introduced in Tibet mainly in connection with the monasteries. For, the wise Buddhist lamas understood that the propagation of religion only by establishing monasteries might not be very fruitful to the illiterate mass of Tibet, mainly the 'rough population of shepherds living in the bitter mountains of Western Tibet'. Hence they adopted the device of decorating the temples with paintings, sculptures and statues made out of a mixture of paper, most probably the torn leafs of the sacred books, cloth and clay, all unique in their character and highly symbolic from the point of view of religion. These arts were done either by the priests themselves who had to learn the arts thoroughly as courses of study or under the able supervision of the learned priests.

In this respect the attention of the learned readers may be invited to Tucci's record and observation of the temple art of Tsaparang monastery situated in Western Tibet (*Indo-Tibetica*, Vol. III: Part 2). There are six temples in the complex. These are described in the afore said book as follows: first is the temple of samvara, the central deity of the temple situated on the top of a steep clay hill at the centre of the royal palace.

Then down the castle there is the small temple of Vajrabhairava (Rdo-rje-hjigs-byed). It is also known as the temple of the AsceticGrub-thob-lha-khan perhaps, because some famous ascetic used to stay there. Then there is the white temple about which Tucci says "It is the real royal temple where the pious dynasty had profusely bestowed its riches". Next is the Red temple at the foot of the hill. At the centre of the temple the Buddha is seated in the posture of *dhyāna*. These two temples are so called due to the color of their walls. Then at a little distance there is the temple of the Prefect. Last is the Lo-than-dgon-pa i.e. the temple of the Lo-tsa-ba in the plains. The present study is restricted to the iconographic manifestations in the Tsaparang monastery which Prof. Tucci has seen almost in a dilapedated condition. From those temples which are 'condemned to inevitable ruins' he recovered the most precious specimens of Tibetan art which, no doubt, borrowed from the Indian Buddhist art of Ajanta and Ellora, show of course, a slow process of acclimatisation.

Buddism had penetrated the Land of Snow in many ways, through Nepal, Kashmir and Central Asia. Technically of course, Buddhism had occurred through many ways from India. It is but natural that like the Buddhist scriptures, Buddhist art also exerted much influence upon the Tibetan art. The mainland style, very naturally was not accepted as such, but had been locally influenced at every stage and introduced in Tibet with a final modification creating a new convention. The classical cave paintings of Ajanta was given an occult touch in Tibet due to the already known precepts of Tantra. The profuse decorative elements such as flowers especially 'Padma', as a decorative floral motif, creepers of various types, birds and animals had no scope in the temple art of Tibet though 'padma' has been extensively used as a religious symbol. Indian Tantricism exhibits a deep aesthetic sense by adopting 'Padma' as one of the basic symbols. For, it grows up from the darkness of filth and mud, comes to the surface of water and raises itself above the water remaining untouched by the things in which it is born. In this way the mind through *sadhana*, unfolds its qualities like the petals of a lotus and raises itself 'beyond the turbulent flow of passions and ignorance and transforms the dark powers of the depth into the radiance of the right knowledge'. A *sādhaka* born in this world, surpasses it. His passions with which he is born remains deeply rooted in the world of ignorance, but on winning over the passions he wakes up into the deepest and the biggest which is symbolised by 'padma'. 'This symbol combines in itself both the material and the spiritual worlds, the individual limited by time and space and the limitless universal, 'the form and the formless, bondage and liberation, the unity between the microcosm and the macrocosm.'

In some of the paintings again, 'the typical Indian attitude of fear for the void' as Tucci interprets it, is seen by filling up the empty space with small figures (*plate no. 1*) shows the image of heruka preserved in the Tibetan Painted Scrolls, (Than Kas). Similar painting are also found at Tsaparang.

Indian influence is also evident in the wooden roof, door and the sculpted pillars of the red temple. Tucci informs us that the roof is very colourful, though the picture that we get is in black and white. The pillars of the door are sculpted from top to bottom. Tucci informs that the 'pillars are sculpted with floral motifs and covered up with small figures worked out with great delicacy', but now a great part is scraped off by the centuries and the inclemencies of weather (*plate no. 2*).

Most prominent however, is the influence Kashmir on the Tibetan art. It may be due to the geographical vicinity. But there is controversy on this point. However, it is especially evident in the wooden *maṇḍalas* of Tsaparang. The biography of Rin-Chen-Zan-Po informs us that this ardent missionary went to Kashmir for several times and brought along with him about seventy-two artisans from Kashmir. The miniature deities of the *maṇḍalas* with slim figures and sharp features were made by the Kashmiri artisans out of the rose wood in the land of Kashmir itself, and afterwards carried to Tibet and placed on the *maṇḍalas* according to necessity. It may be mentioned here that the goddesses either painted or curved with their soft pose bear the distinctive feature of Kashmir school of art. But the most portruding eyes are absent in the Tibetan art. However, these wooden *maṇḍalas* were durable and portable (*plate no. 3*). The plates have been taken from the Tibetan painted scrolls (Than Kas) the similar ones to which Tucci has found at Tsaparang.

These *maṇḍalas*, Tucci finds of utmost 'interest and importance' because of their variation, decoration, colour combination and symbolism. Not a single one is similar to the other. It is interesting to note that most of the deities in the *maṇḍalas* or in the wall paintings stand in *alidha* posture and some in *pratyalidha alidha* posture has been described in the *nātyśāstra* as:

> *asyaiva dakṣinaṁ pādam pañcatalam prasārya tu*
> *ālīdham sthānakaṁ kuryād rudrasyādhi-daivatam.*

It is a typical posture of *tāṇḍava* where the right leg is stretched by five *talas* and the left one remains contracted. These postures are generally used in rasas like *vira*, raudra and *bhayānaka*. Hence, it is obvious why most of the deities stand in these postures (*plate no. 4*).

In some panels there are processions of small female figures of different postures and exquisite grace. Perhaps these were from the brushes of the Indian masters (*plate no. 5*). In the plate the diety to the third from the right stands in *maṇḍala sthānaka* where the legs remain four *tālas* apart. The legs being bent make a circle.

Prof. Tucci very frequently mentions the colour harmony of the temple art. All the plates given in the *Indo-Tibetica*, except two are in black and white. Of these two plates in colour one is a 'terracotta triptych of Indian origin' and the other is one of the twenty-four protectors of the *vajrakaya* (*plate no. 6*). This is in *pratyālīḍha* posture, the opposite of the *alidha*. The male figure is coupled with his *Śakti*. The *Śakti* is in yellow colour, perhaps in yellow ocre, against the background of the greenish black of the male figure as it appears from the picture. The turban of the male figure is in scarlet red and keeping in symmetry with it, there is a red hairband against the blue-black hair of the *Śakti*. The balance of the colour is beautifully maintained by putting the same scarlet red on the bottom of the feet. All the colours are in perfect harmony. The picture shows the rhythm maintained by the out-streteched legs and the two arms while the other two arms are engaged in embrace.

Anyway, it is not possible to give an exhaustive treatment of Tucci's observation and appreciation of all the temple art of Tibet. It will suffice to say that Prof. Tucci saw these temples with more an aesthetic vision than with the eyes of a historian. And it is through the eyes of this real '*sahṛdaya*' that we also see these temple arts of Western Tibet.

Bibliography

1. *Indo-Tibetica*, Vol. III.-Tucci, Guiseppe, Satapitaka Series, 1989.

2. *Tantric Tradition,* Bharati Agehananda, 1970.

3. *Natya Sastra of Bharatamuni*, ed.by Bakuk Nath Sastri & Baladeva Upadhyaya, Chowkhamba Skt. Series, 1985.

Professor Tucci: An Orientalist

6

Biswanath Banerjee

Professor Giuseppe Tucci has been generally known as a Tibetologist of great standing, an Indologist with remarkable achievements, an exponent of Chinese philosophy and religious history, but his enthusiasm in archaeological expeditions as an explorer took him out time and again from the four walls of libraries. His amazingly active life was devoted to study and know Asian countries, to understand the Asian people, to project their history, culture and religion in correct perspectives. In his manifold activity he seems to have been prompted and inspired by his concept of an Eurasian continent, his idea about the unity of the two continents, Asia and Europe, by his belief in a common heritage linking Asia to Europe. A sure and resolute leader with vast experience he used to move from one end of Asia to the other to bring out the truth that 'culture can unite even when politics seems to divide' and project the ideal of human solidarity. An outstanding scholar of incomparable talent Professor Tucci adorned the field of Oriental Studies not only by his innumerable authoritative academic contributions but also by his expeditions and explorations bringing to light number of academic treasures and objects. A fervent promoter and organizer of Oriental

Studies he founded the famous IsMEO in Rome in 1933 and brought it up with great care to strengthen the cause of Oriental Studies. Any interested scholar visiting the Library of the Institute will be amazed to examine it's collections with the rarest of books of great importance in diverse fields. Its collection of Tibetan Manuscripts and Xylographs are perhaps the richest outside China. The Institute possesses documents of immense historical importance with a centre for excavations and archaeological research and a centre for restoration and research in Oriental Studies. The documentary and photographic records of the expeditions in Tibet have been preserved in the Institute which shall convince any visitor of the stupendous task he undertook for himself with a missionary zeal! For his so many expeditions and explorations the inspiration was within his own self as he once said "If science has driven me on to the arduous and difficult routes of Asia, there can be no doubt that the spur of science complied with my inborn for escape, an instinctive love of space and freedom the whim of fancy and of dreaming that can only be fulfilled far from human society...."

With this instinctive love of space and freedom he had established a communion of his spirit with India when he was just thirty years of age. He first came to India in November 1925 and his tie with India was never severed. Before his passing away in April 1984 during his last days Professor Tucci was occupied with a study of Eros and Thanatos in India! His contact with India started with his coming to Santiniketan where he was sent by the Italian government to introduce the study of Italian language. But his indomitable spirit and enthusiasm to know the unknown did not allow him to rest content with the discharge of his duty only! At that time Santiniketan was perhaps the only place in India where one could pursue comparative research in Buddhism because of the presence of a number of distinguished Indian, Chinese and Tibetan experts, and this young Italian scholar took no time to start collaborating with these experts in various fields of Oriental Studies, particularly Tibetan and Chinese. He took advantage of his stay in the *Āshrama* and had the rare fortune of receiving lessons in Bengali from Gurudeva himself. With Gurudeva he read 'some of his poems, and chiefly *Lipikā*' which impressed him very much, and also Sahitya which he thought to have contained 'some of the most brilliant essays in literary criticism' he had ever read. He found Buddhism receiving great attention in the curriculum of Sanskrit studies in Santiniketan, with Tibetan and Chinese given the same importance as Sanskrit. The young scholar was convinced of Gurudeva's idea about a Greater India 'where the most brilliant and everlasting conquests of her thinkers and her artists had spread their inspiration.' 'Tucci considered the time he spent with the Poet as one of the richest in his life and wrote once that 'these years in which the inspiration of the *Rishi* helped to germinate' in him 'some seeds which perhaps were to give later their fruits.' It may be said that in a way Tucci's stay at Santiniketan was the formative period in the career of a future Oriental Scholar of great standing. He spent six years in India, from 1925 to 1930, in teaching Italian, Chinese and Tibetan at Santiniketan, Calcutta University and sometime at Dacca. During this period he worked on some exemplary critical editions of Buddhist texts which were published later.

With hundreds of significant academic contributions that have appeared in various editions, and often in different languages, of diverse themes and subjects ranging from Sanskrit literature to Tibetan history, from Indian Logic to Chinese Philosophy, from Buddhism to Islamic Culture and Art history, from Brahmanic religion to the religion of Tibet and Buddhist mysticism, Giuseppe Tucci undoubtedly emerges as the greatest Oriental Scholar of our time. A peep into the bibliography of his writings numbering about 360, besides so many small reviews, speeches and miscellaneous writings, covering a period of 73 years, from 1911 to 1983, will give us an idea about the vast range of his interest and field of activity. His academic pursuits always aimed at reaching higher goals either through the study and publication of original un-edited texts or through exploration of places untrodaen before. He always took pride in his nomadic life as a traveller and explorer.

His expeditions to Tibet began in 1929 and continued till 1948. During these expeditions in the unexplored Central and Western regions he collected an enormous number of documentation, literary material and art-objects. He extended his activity in the great Himalayan region by carrying six expeditions to Nepal from 1950 to 1954 bringing to light buried Kingdoms and cultures, in which endeavor again his main theme was the encounter between India and Tibet. His two-fold incitement of science and freedom, to which we have already referred in his own words, took the savant fourteen times to the very roof-top of the world and in the neighbouring regions from Karakorum to Indian jungles, Nepal, Lhasa. In this connection I cannot resist the temptation of quoting him to have an idea of his mind and motive behind these daring adventures and the extreme hardships and sufferings that he had undertaken for the advancement of knowledge: 'Eighteen thousands kilometers on foot in one of the most fascinating lands in the world where man, made humble by the immenseness and the silence, imagines or suspect divin presences everywhere, unseen but certain. And almost eight years spent under canvas, without counting the many weeks spent in the open air in the Indian lowlands, on the slow pilgrimage to the holy places of the religious tradition, wandering in the tropical heat along the winding bank of the paddy-fields; and, when the air was too scorching hot, journeying at night by moonlight and resting by day in the wide shade of the mango trees, in that absolute flatness of the

Indian land, as smooth as a petrified sea, in a straight and perfect union of earth and sky.'

His quest for knowledge took him to the study of Pakistan and West Asia, and in 1955 he started a long season of archaeological expeditions in the Swat Valley, later extended to Afghanistan in 1957 and then to Iran in 1959. During this long period of explorations he was able to collect a large number of material for his study which resulted in important publications by himself and by his colleagues and students, widening our knowledge in history, philosophy and culture of these areas. He had a significant role in the setting up of the Swat Museum, in the re-ordering of the Islamic collections in the Kabul Museum and in arranging the collections of Islamic art in Ghazni. His most outstanding contribution in this area has been leadership in the restoration of the most prestigious centre of ancient Iranian civilization, Persepolis, and of the chief Islamic monuments of Esfahan. His cultural sensivity is brought out of these works which also speak of his interest in Asian culture. He had the urge and desire to do things actually, 'to promote and organise study, to carry out investigations and lead them himself over the paths of Asia that had always remained dear to him'.

His focus of attention behind all his researches and explorations had been *Man* understood 'everywhere, under every sky, in every clime.. as the same creature that suffers, cherishes hope, is elated....! In his study of the religious systems he found man always as the subject of experience in different ways but with similar ideals and aspirations! This profession of humanism of Tucci found expression in his passion for religion and originating in him a deep and absorbing interest in Buddhism, 'the highest expression of Asiatic humanism.'

His best and lasting contributions to Buddhist studies have been editions of un-edited and restorations of fragmentary

Sanskrit texts, translations of important Sanskrit texts lost in their originals but preserved in Tibetan and Chinese translations, editions and translations of Tibetan Chronicles, translations of texts on Chinese history and philosophy, all shedding illuminating light on different aspects of Buddhism. Professor Tucci's writings have added a new dimension to the study of Buddhism and have enriched the study of Indian Logic in general and Buddhist Logic in particular. He brought to light some important Pre-Dinnāga texts on logic by Asaṅga and Vasubandhu from Chinese sources and dealt with the doctrines of Maitreyanatha and Asanga in an illuminating paper. It was Professor Tucci who put Dinnaga, the father of mediaeval India Logic, in a brighter perspective than he was actually held, by his editions of Dinnaga's works and papers on him. His comparative study of the Chinese and Sanskrit versions of the first two chapters of the *Laṅkāvatāra* is a pioneering work of this type. His note on the *Laṅkāvatāra* and the idealistic school in Buddhism, his contributions on Nagarjuna and the *Prajñā-pāramitās* show his deep knowledge of the two most important branches of *Mahāyāna* Buddhism. He has strengthened the study of meditational Buddhism by a critical edition of the three *Bhāvanākramas* of Kamalasila. The *Śatasāstra* of Aryadeva was translated by Tucci from both Sanskrit and Chinese sources with commentary and his own notes. He had also made a study of the Chinese version of the *Catuḥśataka* by Aryadeva comparing it with the Sanskrit text and its Tibetan translation. An excellent edition of *Madhyānta-vidhāga-sūtra-bhāsya-ṭīkā* of Sthiramati was prepared by him jointly with Mm. Vidhusekhara Sastri. *A Sketch of Indian Materialism* by him and his edition of the *Vādavidhi* are two works to understand the Indian school of materialism. He was not occupied only with logic, philosophy, history and religion but had much interest in literary productions as will be evident from his writings on Asvaghosa, Kalidasa, *Purāna-pañcalakṣaṇa, Avadāna, Jātaka, literature of Tibet*, translation of *Karpuramañjarī,* and so on. In two learned articles he has shown his acquaintance with Sri Caitanya and Ramakrsna. In 1921 he published a thought-provoking paper on the influence of Buddhism on the civilization of the extreme Orient and in 1977 he attracted attention of scholars by suggesting New Areas of Research. Young scholars of archaeology and Buddhology will be much benefited to go through his suggestions. His stand as a true scholar of religious thought will be borne out by his *Asia Religiosa* and two other small papers on *Confucius and Lao tse and Lhasa and Lamaism.* His treatises on Tibetan and Chinese studies are so numerous that one can not deal with them is a paper like this! In the volumes entitled *Indo-Tibetica*, published from 1932-1941 he brought to light several important chronicles, literary works and texts on monastic history. The *Ancient Civilization of Transhimalaya* published in 1973 is a mine of information on the culture and civilization of the area based on archaeological findings. An outstanding contribution in Tibetan studies has been his *Deb t'er dmar po gsar ma,* Tibetan Chronicle by *bsod nams grags paī,* published in 1971 with the original Tibetan text, emendations to the text, English translation and an appendix containing two minor Chronicles. His *Religions of Tibet* published in 1970 in four languages, German, Italian, French and English is perhaps the best work on the subject till now. His *Tibetan History of Buddhism in China* and *Discovery of the Mallas* are two informative treatments on China and Nepal. Though he published some glosse upon the *Guhyasamāja* as early as in 1935 it was during the latter part of his career that the savant found later or the Tantrik phase of Buddhism as of absorbing interset. The theory and practice of the Mandala, published in Italian, French and English in 1949 and *Rati-līlā*, an interpretation of Tantric imagery of the temples of Nepal in English, French and German (1969) speak of his deep understanding of this phase of Buddhism. He had made a study of the *Kālacakra* system, the latest phase of Buddhism, from Sanskrit and Tibetan sources, and wanted to edit and translate the voluminous Sanskrit text the *Vimalaprabha*. Unfortunately for us he could not fulfil his mission! The three-volume *Tibetan Painted Scrolls* published in 1949, may be considered his Magnum opus, however, exhibits his mastery over the intricacies of later mysticism which has made the last phase of Buddhism not only different to the utmost, but sometimes confusing even! His understanding of the subject and its presentation in an impressive manner have solved for us, not all but many, knotty problems of Tantra study in general and Buddhist Tantricism in particular. He based his study on a large number of published and unpublished materials including the pictorial representations of the various mood, idea or topics as in the Tibetan *tankas*. Of particular value and importance is his treatment of Tibetan mterials in this work in making up a history of the origin and development of the Vajrayana including an attempt to project the importance of the *Kālacakra* system. Though it has not been possible to trace the history conclusively he has certainly made a beginning and has shown and paved the way for us. He has explained how some Tantric cycles arose precisely on India's extreme boundaries, some even outside Indian territory. It seems he has gone through available Sanskrit materials, critically studied the significance of a large number of *taṅkās* and Tibetan art-materials, and has ransacked Tibetan chronicles including the writings of mk' as grub C'os re (1385-1438), *Tson K'a pa, Pad ma kar po*, Cilu pa, Vibhuti Candra, to name only a few, to find out the history of the *Vajrayāna* and *Kālacakrayāna* which exercised a potent influence on the life, culture and religion of Tibet. This voluminous work is a monumental creation, and by its contents, significance and importance has remained unsurpassed till today and for which Professor Giuseppe Tucci has been rightly acknowledged as the greatest authority on Tibet.

A Tribute to Giuseppe Tucci

7

C. S. Prasad

On this August occasion of the Centenary Seminar on Giuseppe Tucci and Indological Studies, I would first pay my tribute to Prof. Giuseppe Tucci, a great scholar of Buddhism and Indology. My contact with Prof. Tucci goes back to the Cheena-Bhavana of Visva-Bharati and sent my research paper to him for perusal and favour of publication in the East and West, the esteemed journal of the Istituto Italiano, Roma. In reply he wrote, "I have perused with interest your article on '*Theravāda and Vibhajjavāda*' and shall be glad to have it published in East and West within the course of this year" — 24 March 1968. His approval of my approach and conclusion in the very first research paper gave me so much confidence that ever since I had not had to look back. In 1970 I left Santiniketan for Tokyo University, Tokyo and therefrom returned to the Nava Nalanda Mahavihara, Institute for teaching and research in Pali and Buddhism, Nalanda. Here too, there came an opportunity to renew the contact with him when the citation was being prepared for confering on him the honoris cause degree of *Vidyā Vāridhi* (D.Litt.) of the Mahavihara on 16 April 1978. In fact the Mahavihara honoured itself by honouring him.

Personal contact with Prof. Tucci has inspired me a great deal, though my field of specialisation is early Buddhism, particularly critical and comparative study of Pali texts with their Chinese counterparts, and I felt his absence in this field of study ever today. His absence is quite understandable. While still he was in his twenties, the most productive period of study in Pali in Europe had come to near completion. It was not that the last word on the life and teachings of Buddha embodied in Pali scriptures was said and there remained nothing for other to do. From the very beginning the Buddhist stúdies in Europe have been oriented more towards philological and grammatical problem. J.W. De Jong has observed, "the West has been nurtured in a long tradition of editing, translating and analysing Latin and Greek texts. The methods developed by classical scholars have been applied to the study of Sanskrit and Pali texts."

Before T. W. Rhys Davids returned to England resigning from the Ceylon Civil Service in 1872, the Pali studies had gone a long way to bear fruits. Viggo Fausball first published the Roman transcription and Latin transcription of the *Dhammapada* in 1855, and then the Jataka tales during 1861-72. Robert Childers was also a member of Ceylon Civil Service. He left the job in 1964 and returned to England in order to concentrate on his *Pali-English Dictionary* which came out in two volumes in 1872 and 1875. Eugene Burnough in collaboration with Christian Lassen published the first scholarly work, *Essai sur la Pali*, and also a text on Pali grammar in 1827. He was a product of collage de France. George Turnover published the text and translation of the Pali Chronicle, *Mahāvamsa* in 1837 which proved to be a valuable source for historians and archaeologists. Following him, James Princep identified the Devanampiya of the *Mahāvamsa* with the king Asoka. In 1879 Hermann Oldenberg edited another Pali chronicle *Dipavaṁsa* and in 1889 he published the *Buddha,*

His Life, His Doctrine, His Community in which he presented the Buddha as a historical figure stripped of legendary details. This subtraction method of Oldenberg was opposed to that of Senart who saw in the legendry mythological stories woven around a coherent system coming from even before the time of the Buddha.

These efforts made in Pali studies by scholars of different countries of Europe were disconcerted, individual based. Rhys Davids brought these scholars together under the auspices of the Pali Text Society established in 1881. His efforts gained momentum and the Pali studies dominated the academic scenario of Europe. Four decades later when Rhys Davids died in 1922, the Society had the credit of publishing "the whole of canonical texts, a large number of Pali commentaries, about a dozen translations and some issues of a journal containing learned articles on Buddhism and on the Pali language and literature."

But the Pali studies from a small part of Buddhist studies with the difference that Pali texts belong to a particular school of early Buddhism, Theravada, whereas the Buddhist texts available from other sources like Sanskrit, hybrid-Sanskrit, Chinese and Tibetan, were of different early Buddhist schools and later schools of Mahayana. Theravada, its tradition and literature has come down uninterrupted and intact while other schools ceased to exit centuries ago and their scripture were lost or went unnoticed, except those translated into Chinese and Tibetan. Even the original of the Mahayana scriptural texts were not readily available, they were to be hunted out.

B.H. Hodgson, British resident in Nepal (1821-43) was the pioneer in making available Sanskrit manuscripts to Sanaskrit scholars in Europe. During his stay in Nepal he searched out several dozens of such manuscripts and sent them to the libraries of London, Paris and Calcutta. This drew the attention of scholars to Sanskrit Buddhist texts. Burnough turned to the study of these manuscripts of Hodgson and devoted the rest of his life to them. A contemporary of Buronough was Kern who was noted for denying the historical existence of the Buddha.

Search for manuscripts was taken seriously and during the last decade of the 19th century, and in the first quarter of the 20th century several expeditions were organised by Sir Aurel Stein (1862-1943), Grunwedel (1856-1935), George Huth (1867-1906), P. Pelliot (1878-1945) and others. Their efforts witnessed a boom in coming out to Europe Buddhist manuscripts in Sanaskrit, Kuchan Khotanese and so on. These manuscripts and presence in them of different editions of some texts like Dhammapada and fragments of Sanskrit *Agama sutras* further accelerated the work of editing and translation. The possession of exegetical and philosophical texts like *Abhidharmakosa* of *Sarvastivada* school, *Vimsika* and *Trinsika* broadened the scope of Vijnanavada school, Logical works of Dignaga, Dharmakirti and Dharmottara broadened the scope of philosophical studies. Attempts were being made to understand the scholsatic Buddhism and the process of development of Buddhist thought. Sinologists like Ramaset, Julian, Beal and Thomas had showed the importance of Chinese materials in the study of Indian Buddhist history through their translations of the records of Chinese travelers. The importance of Chinese and also Tibetan was recognised in the study of *Sutras* and *Sastras*. Buddhist studies became gradually complex requiring knowledge of Sanaskrit, Pali, Chinese, Tibetan above the fair knowledge of the subject.

The sixties of the 19th century witnessed the births of several eminent scholars of Indology and Buddhism. They were Sylvain Levi (1863-1925), Th. Stcherbasky (1866-1942), E.J. Thomas (1869-1958), Louis da la valle Poussin (1869-1938), Heinrich Luder (1869-1943) and others. Each opened a new vista of Buddhist studies and were on the forefront when Prof.

Tucci entered the arena. He as a successor had the benefit of the understanding of his predecessors but he had also a cut over other to become different from others. His master over the language of source materials stood him a good stead. He entered into every field and excelled. He made a number of expeditions and visits to Nepal and to unexplored regions of Western and Central Tibet and collected a good amount of literary and art materials. On his last expedition to Tibet he succeeded in producing two thousand years old manuscripts of which he had just an inkling. He was a prolific writer and versatile scolar. He edited and translated Dignaga's *Nyayamukha. His Pre-Dignaga Buddhist texts on logic from Chinese sources* and other articles on logical problems are supposed to be his special contribution to Buddhist philosophy.

The other aspect of his contributions to be taken note of in his works on Tibet. Tibet is not easily accessible and so are its religion Lamaism and people. No amount of theoretical knowledge can help one to understand Lamaism and its culture perfectly well unless one lives together with keen eye and appreciative attitude. Ippolito Desideri (1684-1733) came to Lhasa in 1715 and lived there learning Tibetan for years. Prof. Tucci was very much impressed by the exactness of his description of religion and culture of Tibet, published late in 1904. In his *Religion of Tibet, Tibetan Folk Songs, Tombs of the Tibetan Kings,* and other works, Prof. Tucci has gone far ahead in doing justice to the subject.

Prof. Tucci led excavation team to Afghanistan and Pakistan. Here in memoriam Prof. Tucci, I may divert to some queries about the ancient Nalanda Mahavihara. The earliest literary sources to Nalanda are the Pali scriptures, their counter Chinese Agamas and the Jain Agamas. But the material available are not only meagre but also short in covering span of time, the life time of the Buddha only. Nalanda was on the outskirt of the capital town of Rajagrha. While the Buddha was living, the king Ajatasatru decided to shift the capital to Pataliputra. A good number of punched mark coins found on the surface in recent times shows that the place was deserted all at once. With Rajagrha, Nalanda also fell in oblivion.

The other literary sources to Nalanda are the records of the Chinese travellers. Fa-xian (399-414) passed through the village of Nala and paid homage to the birthplace of Sariputra, one of the foremost disciples of the Buddha. The king Asoka erected a stupa there. He did not make any reference to the Nalanda Mahavihara. His silence has been interpreted to mean that it was then not in existence. Xuan-zang recorded that the site for the Nalanda Mahavihara was selected by Augury and Kumar Gupta I of the Gupta dynasty, who is also known as Sakraditya (A.D.415-55); constructed the first *Vihara* and his successors one after another added more viharas to it. A question here arises as to why the king selected a remote place far way from the capital city of Pataliputra, for developing a monastic-cum-academic establishment. If it was selected out of love for education, art and culture, the old monasteries of the fame of Asokama at Pataliputra would have been easily accessible. The answer will have its bearing on the beginning of monastic education at Nalanda. Whether it was initiated by the state or whether the state just came forward to give patronage to the existing one which had taken a viable shape before/by his time. If we opt for the latter possibility, the question remains as to why and how Nalanda developed into an academic centre of such a repute.

The Tibetan accounts which are comparatively later recorded that Nagarjuna the propounder of the Madhyamika school of Buddhist philosopy was the first lord Abbot of Nalanda Mahavihara. He flourished sometime in the 2nd century during the region of Satavahana. He was succeeded by his illustrious disciple Aryadeva. Given credence, it may be visualised that the Acarya Nagarjuna on his rounds of holy places happened to be at Nalanda, the birthplace of Sariputra, and took fancy to stay at the halting place one erected for the Buddha. The attraction and the place gradually turned into a centre of academic discussions and discourses. In this light Hui-li's remark in the Life of Xuan-zang, makes a sense that since seven hundred years back the monks of the monastery were not found guilty of breaking the disciplinary rules.

The ruins of the Nalanda Mahavihara is massive and archaeological finds are in a big bulk. But these are the legacy of Pala period dating back to 9th century. The layers of 6th and 7th centuries have also been marked by the excavators, but no architectural design has come to light. When we refer to Nalanda, we have in mind the description of Xuan-zang. But where is Nalanda of Xuan-zang's description? Mary L. Stewart, the author of Nalanda Mahavihara: *A Study of an Indian Pala period Buddhist Site and British Historical Archaeology*, 1861-1938, London, 1989, thinks of some other site at Nalanda. But there is no other site but the excavated one. Cunningham identified Nalanda and its site but the later excavators do not seem to have kept Xuan-zang's description in mind. There is an urgent need to locate the complexes of Kumar Gupta I and his successors and if it is done, it will help to locate other important sites like Mulagantha kuti and the others.

'Last but not the least, there is a question relating to the destruction of old Nalanda Mahavihara. It is said that it was set on fire by Ikhtiyar Khilji in 1199 and the complexes particulartly three libraries continued burning for several months. Archaeological evidences to this effect are not sufficient to prove anything. Did Nalanda Mahavihara met a natural death, through aging and lost of vigour, not unlike Buddhism itself in India and the Turkish invasions simply hastened the process comming back to Prof. Tucci, I feel he himself is a message to Buddhist Scholars.

Giuseppe Tucci and Tibetan Buddhism

8

Pranabananda Jash

Giuseppe Tucci one of the excellent exponents of Tibetan religion and culture (b. June 5,1894 d. April 5,1984) expressed his ideas on Tibetan Buddhism on the basis of his experience, exploration and other contemporary records. His writings on the history of Buddhism in Tibet is still considered as a classical one. Dharmasvamin and Taranatha, the two Buddhist monks from Tibet of the thirteenth and sixteenth century A.D. respectively, afford us adequate information relating to the history of Buddhism in Tibet during their time. After an interval of six-seven centuries Tucci, besides Rahul Samkirtayana, explored the land of snow and vividly described the condition and position of this faith in the tiny surrounding of Trans Himalayan range. Most of his writings on Buddhism or its allied subjects are the presentation of the history and peculiarities of Tibetan Buddhism which reflects, more or less, the history and evolution of *Mahāyāna* Buddhism with little modifications for indigenous needs.

Tibetan Buddhism since its introduction in the first half of the seventh century A.D. played a vital and significant role for the development in almost every facet of the Tibetan history. Lama Anagarika Govinda explains the mystic rituals of Tibetan

Buddhism.[1] But in the subsequent period profoundly Buddhist in all aspects of its social, cultural and religious life, it was, until 1959, dominated by the monastic impact and hierarchy. Tradition avers that Buddhism was introduced into Tibet during the life time of Sroṅ-btsan-sgam-po, who died in 649 A.D., and is held by all schools to be the founder of the Tibetan royal dynasty.[2]

But before the advent of Buddhism in the land of snow a type of animistic religious faith and belief prevailed which has later on left its traces on the later Buddhist development.[3] It is stated that the first king of Tibet "who was the maker of the Tibetan Nation.... married a Nepalese princes about the year A.D. 630; the young bride brought with her, gods and priests; she was given a place in the Tibetan pantheon as an incarnation of the goddess Tara."[4] The same king married a daughter of the Tang emperor T ai Tsong, and she, likewise a Buddhist, was deified in the same way.

Ethnic diversity of this land can not be denied. In fact, the religio-cultural history of Tibet is a conglomeration of various ethnic stocks of different periods. Sum pa mkdam po (1704-1788 A.D) mentions a few legendary ethnic groups like Mu, idong, strong gra, bru.[5] They had their own cultural identity, but they gradually, lost their traditional identity and formed a strong and broad division after the name of Buddha the great, i.e. Buddhism. Moreover, the geographical factor made this tiny land to achieve its historical and cultural aspirations from time to time. Lying on one of the highways from India to China, through Nepal, Tibet was thus naturally from the beginning open to Indian and Chinese influences, and these are distinctly recognizable in religion- the history of Buddhism in Tibet; in Tibetan art, with the development of the Tibetan painted scroll; in architecture with the design of temples, monasteries, *stūpas*; and in politics, with the institution of the Dalai Lama; in social structure, with a large segment of the male population becoming celibate monks; in language, with the creation of the Tibetan scriptures, and in literature, with the composition of thousands of Buddhist texts in a vast variety of genres.

Thus Buddhist thought, practice and institution were imported into Tibet from India sometime in the beginning of the seventh century A.D. developed rapidly by contacts with influential Buddhist figures of Kashmir and northern India. Although Tibetan Buddhist thought mainly inherits from India, there have also been marginal influences from China and Central Asia.[6] G.Tucci has made an indepth study on this issue and he argues that "The Buddhism entering Tibet came not only from India (by which is to be understood not only India proper, but also its border regions Nepal and Kashmir) but also from present day Afghanistan and Gilgit, from the cities along the caravan routes of Central Asia (then known as the Silk routes), and from China. Buddhism has never refused to accept, rework and transform the ideas of other peoples. In these territories bordering on Tibet there existed numerous religious forms in a picturesque juxtaposition which favoured exchange and reciprocal borrowings. The Chinese translations of Nestorian and Manichaean texts borowed technical expressions from Taoist and Buddhist terminology, and indeed they borrowed more then just terminology. *Vajrayāna* (gnostic) Buddhism developed hand in hand with Saivism. It is probable that in these ways, through the meditation of Buddhists influence by other streams of thought or for that matter directly, ideas foreign to Buddhism could be introduced within it, and gradually be merged into a developing doctrinal structure."[7] There is no denying the fact that Tibetan Buddhism as it exists today, is one of the major forms of Buddhism in this subcontinent, with its influence extending far beyond the geographical jurisdiction of Tibet, to the Kalmyk region of Russia near the Caspian Sea in the West, to Siberia in the North, to Mongolia, China, and Manchuria in the East, and to Nepal in the South. This religious tradition may properly be designated as Tibetan Buddhism, rather than Lamaism, a term that erroneously suggests that the religion of Tibet is not Buddhism. Giuseppe Tucci long ago observed that "Lamaism introduced here (Nepal) the habitats of Tibet; but met here with other customs which enjoyed in confirmity with the practices formerly observed in Tibet by some Bon-po, that the corpse should be cast in the rivers. And so the white scarf, still used in the funeral rites of some Bonpo tribes on the boundaries of China, is the emblem of the rope which, in the original shaman form, joined, like a bridge, the earth to the sky and on which the deceased walked up. The old beliefs have not been fully abandoned; a compromise has been reached, and instead of casting the corpse into the river his image is thrown in it."[8] In fact, the word Lama is restricted to a few categories of monks and priests and is not used indiscriminately for all monks and priests. The term Lama means the 'Superior one' and is taken to correspond to Guru who can administer initiation (Dbang, Sanskrit *Dikshā*). A Lama is thus not necessarily an incarnate (Sprul-sku=Sanskrit *Nirmāṇakāya*), while any incarnate is not ipso facto a Lama. The word Lama meaning preceptor or priest was in currency in Tibet before the advent of Buddhism and the priest in the pre-Buddhist Bon religion was, as is still, called Lama. Thus no new coinage was needed to render into Tibetan the Indian term Guru abounding in the *Mahāyāna* literature particularly the treatises and tracts on *Tantra*; there are numerous examples in Kanjur and Tanjur authenticating Lama for Guru.[9] Without a spiritual guide an esoteric system (*Tantra*=Rgyud), as was the form of *Dharma* propagated in Tibet, cannot succeed. Thus Buddhism in Tibet begins with Guru (Lama) and the saviour of Buddhism in Tibet, Padmasambhava, goes down in history as the Guru.

Bon has still retained its own identity to this day. In addition, there remains a vast area of rites and beliefs that are neither specifically Buddhist nor Bon but may be designated "popular religion" or "the religion without a name." G.Tucci points out that "In any case Buddhism must have already, from its first entry into Tibet, undergone much modification and weakening. It cannot be denied that the local cults and beliefs persisted to a large degree, and that there were powerful centres of Bon resistance throughout the country."[10] In fact, the impact of Buddhism on this creed was so strong that the Bon came to have even a Bon Sans-rgyas or Bon Buddha and like the *Dkon-mchog* gsum *(Triratna)*- the *Buddha, Dharma and Sangha* of Buddhism, the Bon developed their own *gyungdrung*, *gsum*, the three *svastikas*. The Bon architecture, iconography and sacred furnishings are much common with those of Tibetan Buddhism. And just as Buddhism transformed the Bon religion, the latter, in turn, infected Buddhism itself for its existence. We see a whole mass of *Du*, and *Nyan Sadhak, thab-lha, pho-lha*, i.e., the black demons, the arglies, the serpent spirits, the hearth gods, the tutelary gods, creeping into the Buddhist pantheon on the Tibetan soil. S.C.Das observed that Padmasambhava was summoned to Tibet from Udyana (Kafiristan) in the eighth century A.D., and in the eleventh century A.D. Pandita Atisa introduced reforms in what must have been a strange admixture of Buddhism, magic and animism.[11] As a result of it the religious scenario in Tibet took a new form which was the outcome of an admixture between the Bon po and the newly advent Buddhism.

Buddhism is traditionally demarcated in terms of two distinct periods- the earlier dissemination of the doctrine started in the second half of the eighth century A.D., while the second one emerged in the later half of the tenth century A.D. The first phase witnessed the translation of Buddhist texts from Sanskrit into Tibetan, the establishment of Buddhist monasteries and the patronage of Buddhism by the royal and the noble families. It ended with the suppression of Buddhism by King Lang Darma in 836 A.D.

The second Buddhist wave in Tibet began over a century later, i.e. in the later half of the tenth century A.D. It was also marked by the translation of many Buddhist texts, exchange of Tibetan and Indian Buddhist monks and teachers, and the lineages of teaching established between India and Tibet ultimately gave rise to the major sects of Tibetan Buddhism.

Whatever may be date of introduction of Buddhism in Tibet, there is hardy any doubt that sustained Tibetan exposure to Buddhist thought and practice began at the end of the eight century A.D., during the reign of King Trisong Detsen, when Santarakshita the reputed Indian Pandita, was invited to Lhasa, the then Tibetan capital. The Buddhist teachings preached by Santarakshita was not acceptable to all, and thus a section of the Tibetan people blamed him for a series of national disasters on the introduction of the foreign faith. The Indian Pandita was forced to retreat of Nepal, but before doing so, he advised the King to invite the Tantrika master Padmasambhava to Tibet. The King agreed, and according to the chronicles written several centuries later, Padmasambhava converted the demons of Tibet to the Buddhist fold, enlisting their promise to always protect the new faith. After sometimes, Santarakshita returned to Tibet, where he joined with Padmasambhava and the King to establish the first Buddhist monastery at *bsam-yas, Samye* (Tibet) in 779 A.D.[12] Where several Tibetans were ordained as the first Buddhist monks, "after the foundation of *bsam-yas* and the official recognition of Buddhism"[13] Padmasambhava remained a strong mythic presence for Tibetan Buddhism.[14] Santarakshita and Padmasambhava were well versed in both Buddhist doctrine and Tantrik form of Buddhism. Through the Tibetan Buddhism tradition these two teachers played important role with the assertions of the various philosophical schools,

Buddhist and non-Buddhist, and also employed their expertise in ritual and in meditation for showing hidden powers.

But a tussle of doctrinal controversy erupted in Tibet when the Chinese Buddhist monks of the Ch'an (zen) school led by one Mo-ho-yen visited the Buddhist monastery at Samye in Tibet.[15] Tradition avers that Santarakshita professed of dangers from the Chinese position and left instructions in his will that his student Kamalasila be called from India to counter the Chinese view. The reason for conflict was over the question of the nature of enlightenment. The Indians held that enlightenment takes place as the culmination of a gradual process of purification, the result of combining virtuous action, meditative serenity, and philosophical insight. The Chinese, on the contrary, believed that enlightenment was the intrinsic nature of the mind rather than the goal of a protracted path, such that one need simply to recognize the presence of this innate nature of enlightenment by entering a state of awareness beyond distinctions; all other practices are superfluous. According to both Chinese and Tibetan records, a debate was held between Kamalasila and Mo-ho-yen at Samye in 797 A.D. with King Trisong Detsen himself serving as judge. The Tibetan accounts (contradicted by the Chinese accounts) mention that Kamalasila defeated Mo-ho-yen, and thus he with his party left Tibet. The King then ordered that the *Mādhyamika* School of Buddhist Philosophy (to which Santarakshita and Padmasambhava belonged) would be followed in Tibet.

A large number of Tibetan monks and scholars visited India, studied at Nalanda and or Vikramasila and went back to their country to preach the spiritual and philosophical aspects of their study. Chag lo-tsa wa-Chos rje-dpal (the translator Dharmasvamin) seems to be the only one among them who left the account of India, her people, customs and institutions.[16] During the pro Buddhist policy of the Malla Kings several youths went to Kashmir to study Buddhist teachings. One of these youths was later to become eminent under the name of Rin chen bzang po (958-1055 A.D.). G. Tucci has pointed out that "Kashmir was an appropriate place not only because of its nearness, but also because the last splendor of the Buddhist schools then held away there, and famous religious teachers preserved both the speculative and logical tradition, and the practice of the Tantra and ritual. At the end of their education, the youths returned from Kashmir to their homeland, along with teachers and also some artists, and they began to propagandize their faith over a wide region under the protection of the court."[17]

In fact, Buddhism expanded through west Tibet and a galaxy of Buddhist scholars from India were invited to Tibet. It is generally believed that "after the death of K'ri sron lde btsan there was a strong revival of Indian Buddhism, caused not only by the direct instigation of the court, anxious to prevent any further Chinese influence, but also by the growing prestige of the Indians and the coming of Indian *ācāryas* in greater number than before. Then Jnanamitra, Jnanendrabodhi, Silendra, Danasila, Bodhimitra, Ratnarakshita, Dharmatasila, Jnanasena, Jayarakshita, Manjusrivarman, Ratnenda rakshita, etc. representing the new trend of Buddhism based on a careful study not only of the law but also of *Vyākarana* and eager to find a strict correspondence between Sanskrit and Tibetan, undertook a great work of translation and revision. In this period, which, if we accept the date contained in the *Sgra sbyor*, covers the reign of K'ri ide sron btsen, the real consolidation of Indian Buddhism took place."[18] Specific conclusion on this point is not beyond doubt; but it is significant that from this point Tibet largely sought its Buddhism from India; and no school of Chinese Buddhism had any further influence in Tibet.

With the patronage of the Tibetan king, Buddhism flourished unprecedently. But the translation of Indian Buddhist literature- the *Sūtras, Śāstras and Tantras*, from Sanskrit into

Tibetan was interrupted by the suppression of Buddhist monastic institution in 838 A.D. The Tibetan monarchy ended shortly thereafter with the assassination of the king who had ordered the closing of the Buddhist monasteries. Internal turmoil and tussle for royal authority in political scenario checked the smooth progress and development of Buddhism for the time being. The status of Buddhist thought and practice during the next century and a half remains only vaguely understood by the scholars.

Thus Buddhism with its zeal and vigour again appeared in the eleventh-twelfth centuries A.D. when Tibetan monks and scholars came to India where they studies with Indian Buddhist teachers in Bihar, Bengal and Kashmir, and many of the sects of Tibetan Buddhism trace their lineages back to these encounters. It may be mentioned in this connection, for examples, that the Kagyupa sect derives its lineage from the visits to India by Marpa the translator (1012-1099 A.D.) where he studies under several Tantrik teachers of the contemporary period, including Naropa and Maitripa. The Sakyapa sect looks back to another translator, Drok mi (993-1050 A.D.) who studied in India under disciples of the Tantrik teacher Virupa. It was Sakyapa scholar Buton Rinchen Drub (1290-1364 A.D.) who systematised the various collections of Indian Buddhist texts circulating in Tibet into the well-known Kanjur (translation of the word of the Buddha) and the Tanjur (translation of the *Sāstras*). The Indian scholars to visit Tibet during the second dissemination was the famous Atisa (982-1054 A.D.) whose followers became the Kadampa sect, regarded as a forerunner of the Gelugpa. It is observed that "His (Atisa's) work had included not only the diffusion of the doctrine which had already been codified, but in particular a new emphasis on the cult of the goddess Tārā, to whom he was especially devoted. He wrote concise texts to serve as introduction to leading on to a more profound study of the Buddhist doctrine of salvation".[19] On the basis of the account of Dharmasvamin, it is stated that "Indian Buddhism had naturally exercised considerable influence over the Tibetan Buddhism in the literary and philosophical spheres. The practice of Tantrika processes and mystic *mandalas*, the worship of deities like Aparājitā, Khasarpaṇa, Avalokiteśvara, Rematā and Blue Achalā and the study of *Pāramitā* works, like *A hṭasāhasrikās* and *Panchavimsati-sāhasrikās* had become very popular".[20] The work of Dharmasvamin also shows that architecture also did not remain uninfluenced. It points out how the court-yard of the Vajrasana temple had gates to the east, north and west but none to the south, and observes that Tibetan temples and monastic courtyards followed the example and did not provide for any gate to the south.[21]

It is to be noted in this connection that during the Mongol Yuan dynasty (1260-1368 A.D.), Tibetan Buddhism played an important role at the court of Kublai Khan, where the emperor's Buddhist preceptor was the famous monk Phags pa (1280 A.D.?) of the Sakyapa sect. Imperial titles were also bestowed on monks of the Kagyupa sect. Chinese emperors in the Ming dynasty (1368-1644 A.D.) continued to confer gifts and titles on Lamas of the Kagyupa, Sakyapa and Gelupa sects. During the Qing (1644-1912 A.D.), however, especially from the time of the Kangxi emperor (1661-1722 A.D.), imperial favour was directed primarily towards the Gelugpas. Under the Qianlong emperor (1736-1795 A.D.), for example, the entire Tibetan Kanjur was translated into Manchu under the direction of the Gelugpa hierarch Jangkya Hutuktu Raipai rdorje (1717-1786 A.D.).

The origin of the Gelugpas (dge lugs pa) is said to have inherited from the tradition of Atisa who arrived in Tibet in 1042 A.D. While dealing with the objective of his teaching, Tucci has pointed out: "The teaching aimed in the first place at the purification of mind (blo sbyong), at the realization of the ethical and esoteric principles of Buddhism. Much less time was devoted to Buddhism's highly developed theoretical side. Essentially this instruction was limited to leading the disciple to a better understanding of his own mind and to the achievement of insight into 'voideness' as the limiting state of things (mthar thug), together with compassion. The thought of enlightenment from the point of view of ultimate reality is equated with 'voidness', while compassion results from the same thought when considered from the standpoint of conventional truth. 'Voidness' is the 'body of essence', compassion the 'body of form.'[22]

Tsong Khapa (1357-1419 A.D.) is one of the most eminent figures of this sect. His contribution to the development cannot be denied. He founded the monastery of dgaldan Ganden (named after the Buddhist heaven *Tushita*) outside of Lhasa in 1409 A.D., and his followers were originally known as the Gandenpas. This eventually evolved to Gelug, 'the system of virtue'. The Gelugpas established large monastic organisations, like universities, institutions throughout Tibet and Mongolia, one of which, Drepung, was the largest Buddhist monastery in the world, with over 13000 monks in 1959.

The main trait of Tsong Khapa's work is the pursuit of consistency among apparently disparate or contradictory elements within Buddhist doctrine. He sought to demonstrate a harmony between *sutra* and *tantra*, between reasoned analysis and contemplative experience, between conventional truth and ultimate truth. He claimed that it could be logically established that there is no contradiction between the validity of worldly categories (such as cause and effect, virtue and nonvirtue), on the one hand, and the fact that those categories were empty, that is ultimately lacking in any kind of intrinsic or independent nature, on the other. He also argued that the logical and systematic analysis of the constituents of experience is essential for the attainment of enlightenment. In these less technical works, he said that all of Buddhist practice could be encompassed under the categories of renunciation, the compassionate aspiration to liberate all beings from suffering and the understanding that all phenomena are devoid of substantion or independent existence. He left a massive corpus of writings on a wide variety of topics, his most famous works being two compendia of practice, one detailing the exoteric path of enlightenment, the Great Exposition of the stages of the path to enlightenment and the other detailing the esoteric of tantric path, the Great Exposition of the stages of *Mantra* (sNgags rin chen po.)

After his death, Tsong Khapa was deified by his followers. With the political ascendancy of the Gelug under the fifth Dalai Lama, the exaltation of his legacy became more widely spread. Just as Padmasambhava is spoken of simply as the 'Precious guru', Tibetans often refer to Tsong Khapa as the Precious lord.

Tibetans share with all Buddhist a belief in a cycle of beginningless rebirth called *Samsāra*, where beings are reborn according to the law of *Karma* belief, virtuous actions, like charity and preserving life, result in happiness in the future, while non-virtuous deeds of body (like murder), speech i.e. lying, and mind (i.e. wishing others ill) result in suffering. The effects of these deeds not only determine where one will be reborn after death. There are six possible places of rebirth: the realms of gods, demigods, humans, animals, hungry ghosts, and hell beings. The state beyond suffering is called *nirvana*. In the early Buddhist tradition, the goal seems to have been for each person to strike for his or her own liberation from rebirth. With the rise of the *Mahāyāna*, the goal was expanded to include the liberation of all beings.

Although the various sects of Tibetan Buddhism derive their monastic regulation from the Indian school known pejoratively as the *Hinayāna* (lesser vehicle), all school of Tibetan Buddhism identify themselves as proponents of the *Mahāyāna* (great vehicle), both in their practice and in their philosophy. Perhaps the most famous feature of the *Mahāyāna* is its emphasis on the *Boddisattva*, a person who makes the compassionate vow to become a *Buddha* in order to lead all being in the universe out of suffering and to the bliss of enlightenment. The term *Bodhisattva* was rendered into Tibetan as "one who is heroic in his or her aspiration to enlightenment."

The *Bodhisattva* who is said to be the physical manifestation of all the compassion of all the *Buddhas* in the universe, *Avalokitesvara*, is the particular object of such reverence in Tibet, where it is believed that this *Bodhisattva* form takes successive human births as the Dalai Lama. *Avalokitesvara* is invoked by the famous *mantra*: *Om Mani Padme Hum* (you who hold the jeweled (rosary) and the lotus (have mercy on us). The *Avalokitesvara* form of *Bodhisattva* is very popular and also depicted in a variety of forms in Tibetan art - two of the most frequent being with one head and four arms; and the other with eleven heads and a thousand arms. The multiple arms are said to represent the Bodhisattva's extraordinary ability to come to the aid of suffering setient beings.

In fact, the main traits of Tibetan Buddhism are to be found after Atisa who introduced the later forms of *Mahāyāna* Buddhism, viz., *Vajrayāna, Mantrayāna, Kālacakrayāna*, and other practices. Thus, the later Buddhist practices in Tibet witnessed the assimilation of the most important development of late Indian Tantrik Buddhism. This practice was considered an esoteric approach to the *Mahāyāna* path whereby time required to achieve Buddhahood could be shortened from the standard length of three periods of countless aeons to as little as three years and three months. The Tantrik scriptures are eloquent enough to instruct the technique for effecting such an extraordinary power through an elaborate system of rites, rituals, meditation, etc. These are all very significant features and symbolic too.

The representations of the erotic and wrathful motifs, where male and female are depicted in sexual union and bull-headed deities, adorned with garlands of human heads, brandish cleavers and skull cups, are the very common elements of Tantrika Buddhism in Tibet. It is believed that *prajñā/shes-rab* (wisdom) and *snyong-rje*/karuṇā (compassion) are the essential components of the Bodhisattva's path to Buddhahood. Wisdom (*Prajñā*), especially the perfection of wisdom, is identified with the female. In Tantra the symbolism is revealed in more explicitly sexual terms, with wisdom as female and method male, their union being essential to the achievement of enlightenment. Buddhist Tantra is said to be the 'Diamond Vehicle' (*Vajrayāna*) because wisdom and method are joined in an adamantine and indivisible union, bestowing Buddhahood quickly. This is the general accepted meaning of the depiction of sexual union.

Similarly, the wrathful depiction of the deities in the Tibetan Buddhist pantheon, also bears adequate significance. It may be the continuation of Tibetan Shamanic origin which were added to Indian Buddhism after its arrival in Tibet. These wrathful deities are described vividly in the Buddhist Tantras. According to the Tantrika scriptures some of these deities are Buddhas and Bodhisattvas in their wrathful aspects, the most famous being Yamantaka, the wrathful manifestation of the Bodhisattva of wisdom, Manjusri. He is popular and favourite tutelary deity of the Gelugpa sect. Some of these wrathful deities have the task of protecting the *dharma* (chhos) or to protect from some malignant forces and untoward exigencies.

Per Kvaeyne thus observed about the Bodhisattva concept and its significance in the subsequent peried: "The choice of *Avalokitesvara* was not made at random. As early as the twelfth or thirteenth century, *Avalokitesvara* had come to be regarded in a form of an ape he had, in ancient times, assumed the role of progenitor of the Tibetan people in order that the teachings of the Buddha might flourish in Tibet in due course; in the form of the great Tibetan king Sron-btsan-sgam-po, who created the Tibetan empire in the seventh century, *Avalokitesvara* had established Buddhism, according to this retrospective view in the land of snow. The Potala palace in Lhasa, the ancient capital, was built in its present form by the fifth Dalai Lama and made his residence; situated on a hill, it symbolically reestablished the pre-Buddhist connection between the divine king and sacred mountain"[23]. It thus shows that the incarnation of *Avalokitesvara* i.e. the Dalai Lama became the temporal authority over all sects beside being the spiritual authority over the people of other sects like the Gelugpa or the Yellow Hat sect.

In order to appease the deities the Tibetan Buddhist makes daily practices of worship to a Buddha, a *Bodhisattva*, or a particular deity, and an image of that deiy was therefore employed for that purpose. As mentioned earlier the representations of wrathful deities were believed to offer protection to their owners; various deities whose power were of the more mundane variety, such as, the god of wealth, were depicted and venerated for the boons they could bestow. As per the Tibetan practices images were not considered merely symbolic representations, because each statue and thangka after its completion would be consecrated, in the belief that the principle of enlightenment called the chossku *Dharmakāya* (Truth Body of the Buddha) would come to inhabit the image. In the case of statues, the consecration ceremony required that the inside of a hollow image be filled with scrolls of mantras and various sacred substances and then sealed. It is believed that it will be considered most inauspicious if any one opens the bottoms of such statues and empty out their contents.

It is, however, to be noted that the Panditas or monks whose lives were spent largely in the performance of Tantrika ritual or in various forms of meditation, in an effort to manifest a fantastic world of benign and malevolent forces, propitiating deities and repelling demons, by performing Tantrika instructions on techniques for drawing mandalas, making rain, stopping diseases like smallpox, snake-bites, etc., and manufacturing magical pills.

In an excellent article on '*A Tibetan Classification of Buddihst Images according to their Style*'[24] Tucci expressed his deep understanding on the history of the Buddhist plastic art as well as the metaphysical aspect of these manifestation. The representation of different categories of ***Buddhas*** and *Bodhisattvas* is not without any philosophical significance. The self creative Adi-Buddha creates by thought of the Dhyani-Buddhas who live in perpetual *Nirvāna* with a *Dharma-kaya*, body of Truth-essence, not a physical body. From the *Dharmakāya Buddhas* emanate the *Sambhogakāya Bodhisattvas* and from them in turn the *Nirmanakāya Mānushi Buddhas*. Sambhoga is experience of infinite happiness. In Buddhism, however, the term has been transformed from its ordinary meaning of carnal pleasure to spiritual beatitude. Whereas the Dhyani- Buddha's live in meditation, the Dhyani Bodhisattvas experience supreme happiness, not through the medium of senses, but in mind state. It is, however, believed that once in every *kalpa* (world cycle) they do assume *Nirmāṇakāya*, a mortal frame built of the elements, viz., earth, water, air, fire, etc. Gautama Buddha is regarded as the manushi-Buddha of the present, the fourth cycle, and Avalokitesvara, its Dhyani-Bodhisattva, creator. In the Tibetan tradition there are five Dhyami-Bodhisattvas in the Trikaya system:

1. *Kun-tu-bzan-po* (Samanta Bhadra) - the all benign;
2. *Phyag-na-rdo-rje* (Vajrapāṇi) - the bearer of thunderbolt;

3. *Phyag-na-rin-chen* (Ratnapāṇi)-the jewel-bearer;
4. *Spyan-ras-gzigs* (Avalokitesvara) of compassionate look; and
5. *Phyag-na-sna-tshoga-rdo-rje* (Visvapāṇi vajra) - crossed thun derbolt bearers.

Several other Bodhisattvas, like *Byams-pa* (Maitreya), *bijam-dpal* (Manjuśrī), *Nam mkha snying po* (Ākāśagarbha), *as'i suying po* (Kshitigarbha), *jig rten rnam rgyal* (Trailokya-vijaya), etc. representing various aspects of divinity, such as, love, compassion, beatitude, strength, domination are also prevalent. Female Bodhisattvas are not unknown. They were worshipped by the people for various purposes. Thus Dbyans - Canma (*Sarasvatī*) associated with learning and fine arts; Nor-rgyun ma (*Vasudharā*) with abundance; *Shes-rab-kyi-pha-rol-tu-phyin-pa* (*Prajñāpāramitā*) with transcendental wisdom and others are endowed with various power and attributes.

Bodhisattvas having emanated from a higher state, or having risen from the imperfect state of ordinary men to that of *Arhat*, are fully qualified to become Buddhas. The Bodhisattvas choose not "to disappear like a flame freed form name and form". They sacrifised for the liberation in the midst of suffering humanity sharing their experiences as incarnations and lifting them from their *lot-karman, karuṇā* or compassion gains supremacy over self-centered individual *moksha* or release. In fact, the core of the entire Tibetan attitude to life, in conformity with this ideal, is *karuṇā*, their spiritual leader the Dalai Lama is *karuṇā's* incarnation per excellence. He dominates by the power of love through the conquest of the heart. Another important incarnation is Panchen Lama representing *Hod-dpag-med* or *Amitābha*-infinite light-the *Dhyāni-Buddha* of the existing *kalpa*. Moreover, there are several incarnate *Lamas* called Tulkus who are believed to be incarnations of accomplished Indian, Tibetan or Mongolian saints. The concept of Lama in Tibetan Buddhism occupies a significant role in the spiritual tradition of the order of monks. Tucci in course of his itinerary in various Buddhist monasteries in Tibet met with the Lamas, Tulkus and Panchen Lamas and left an account of them with elaborate description.

In fact, there has been little development or transformation of Tibetan Buddhism in the realm of philosophical ideas but the political domination that the monasteries gradually obtained was without precedent.[25] A uniquely Tibetan feature of monastic role was succession by incarnation the head of an order, or of a monastery, being regarded as the re-incarnation of his predecessor. In other cases, a religious figure might be regarded as the manifestation of a deity or a particular aspect of deity. The Tibetan religious literature testifies to the spiritual authority and temporal immunities of the Lamas. In the person of the fifth Dalai Lama (1617-1682 A.D.) both ideas were combined.[26] Each Dalai Lama was already regarded as the incarnation of his predecessor; the fifth, who established himself as Head of the Tibetan State, also came to be regarded as the emanation manifestation of the great Bodhisattva Avalokitesvara (*Tib.Spyan-ras-gzigs*), as have all subsequent Dalai Lama down to the present one, the fourteenth Dalai Lama:

1. Gedun Truppa	A.D. 1391-1475 A.D.
2. Gedun Gyatso	A.D. 1475-1543 A.D.
3. Sonam Gyatso	A.D. 1543-1588 A.D.
4. Yenten Gyatso	A.D. 1589-1617 A.D.
5. Ngawang Lobzang Gyatso	A.D. 1617-1682 A.D.
6. Tsangyang Gyatso	A.D. 1683-1706 A.D.
7. Kezang Gyatso	A.D. 1708-1757 A.D.
8. Jampel Gyatso	A.D. 1758-1805 A.D.

9.	Luntok Gyatso	A.D. 1806-1815 A.D.
10.	Tshultrim Gyatso	A.D. 1816-1837 A.D.
11.	Khedrup Gyatso	A.D.1838-1856 A.D.
12.	Trinle Gyatso	A.D. 1856-1875 A.D.
13.	Thupten Gyatso	A.D. 1876-1933 A.D.
14.	Tenzin Gyatso	A.D. 1935

The immense power and authority of the Lama in society and government regarding as ' the one with none above'. And this is distinctly reflected in the religous doctrine of Tibetan Buddhism where 'Refuge in Three gems' is not enough and the recitation thus incorporates the Lāmā as the first refuge :

I take refuge in the *Lāmā*
I take refuge in the *Buddha*
I take refuge in the *Dharma*
I take refuge in the *Saṅgha*

The Dalai Lama, as the incarnation of Avalokiteśvara, became the Real Refuge or Precious Protector for all the Tibetan *Nang-pas* (the Buddhas) irrespective of their Sectarian affiliations and territorial loyalties.

References

1. Lama Anagarika Govinda, *Foundations of Tibetan Mysticism*, London, 1959.

2. Giuseppe Tucci, *The Religions of Tibet*, (translated from the German and Italian by Geoffrey Samuel) First paper back printing, University of California press, p.1; *Tibetan Painted Scrolls*, Rome, 1949.

3. S.C.Das, *Indian Pundits in the Land of Snow*, 1893 (first published and reprinted in 1965). Nirmal Chandra Sinha, *Tibet-Considerations on Inner Asian History*, Firma K.L. Mukhopadhya Calcutta, 1967

   S.C.Das, *A brief sketch of the Bon religion, Journal of Buddhist Text Society of India*, I, 1893, Hackin, p 116-17.

4. A.K.Comaraswamy, *History of Indian and Indonesian Art*, 1965, New York, p. 147

5. *Dpag bsam ljon bzang*, Calcutta, 1902, p.148

6. But Robert B. Ekvall, *Religious Observances in Tibet: Patterns and Function*, University of Chicago Press, 1964 often ignores the Indian background and seeks to find in China the meaning of Tibetan religious observances. His sexamination and explanation of what the word chos ('religion') comprehends in the context of Tibetan conceptualisation and thought is an example of this imbalance. Sinha (*Tibet-Considerations on Inner Asian History*, p. 49 ff.) points out the bare 'basic lacuna' of the work of Ekvall and offers an alternative explanation which is more convincing and acceptable.

7. G.Tucci, *op. cit.*, p.15, N.K. Singh (*op.cit.*, p.46) has convincingly shown that - The development of Mahayana in Swat-Gilgit- Pamirs and the emergence of Tantric deities and rituals in these areas would be more relevant to history of Buddhism in Tibet than the work of Indian Pandits in China.

8. G.Tucci, *Preliminary Report on Two Scientific Expeditions in Nepal, Rome*, 1956, Serie Orientale Rome, vol. X, pt. I, p.27 In this connection we may mention that *The Ancient Civilization of Transhimalaya*, which is an English translatism of his Tibet, both published in 1993, deals with the archaeological materials on Tibet, emphasising for the first time on the prehistoric implements of the region.

9. N.K.Sinha, *op. cit.*, p.36

10. G.Tucci, *The Religions of Tibet*, p. 15.

11. S.C.Das, *Indian Pandits in Tibet*, *Journal of Buddhist Texts Society of India*, I, 1893

12. Biography of Dharmasvamin, ed. by G.Roerich, K.P.Jayaswal Institute.

13. G.Tucci, *Minor Buddhist Texts*, Delhi, 1986, p.336.

14. *Ibid*, p. 334-35.

15. B.Lipton and N.Dorjee Ragnubas, *Treasures of Tibetan Art*, Oxford, 1996, p.20.

16. G.Tucci, *Minor Buddhist Texts*, Delhi, 1986, p.318
17. *Ibid.*, p.362
18. G.Tucci, *The Religions of Tibet*, p.21
19. G.Tucci, *Minor Buddhist Texts*, Delhi, 1986, p.360. *The Religions of Tibet*, p.22; cf. also Aloka Chattopadhyaya, *Atisa and Tibet*, New Delhi, 1986.
20. *Biography of Dharmasvamin* (Chag lo-tsa-ba Chos-rje-dpal, a Tibetan Monk pilgrim by Dr. G. Rocrich, K.P.Jayaswal Institute, Patna, p.iii.
21. *Ibid.*, p.73.
22. G. Tucci, *The Religions of Tibet*, p.23
23. *Encyclopedia of Religion*, Mircea Eliade (ed.), vol. 14, 1987, p. 500 ff.
24. *Artibus Asiac*, XXII, 1959, p. 179-187; cf also *Indian paintings in Western Tibetan Temples*, in Artibus Asiac, VII, 1937, p. 191-204.
25 In his Magnum opus-Storia della Filosofia indiana (1957) G Tucci has expressed his ideas about Philosophy.
26. G.Tucci, *Sino-Indian Studies*, 'The Fifth Dalai Lama as a Sanskrit Scholar, vol.V,1957, p. 235-40. For an indepth study please consult C.J Tambiah's book *World Conqueror of World Renonneer* (1984).

Professor Tucci and His School of Italian Sanskritists

9

Indrani Das

Giuseppe Tucci created around himself an atmosphere of oriental scholarship. His contemporary Orientalists in some way were all influenced by him because Prof. Tucci was an authority in his field and there was a constant exchange of ideas between them. Tucci, like his teacher Formichi knew very well several modern Indian languages apart from the classical languages like Sanskrit, Pali, Prakrit and Tibetan. Tucci had read thoroughly the whole *Vaisnava Padavali* in Bengali, as he himself writes to Tagore in one of his letters. He liked very much the *Padavali* of Chandidas.

Around Professor Tucci gathered brilliant scholars interested in Orientalistic Studies. He inspired his friends and disciples to master modern Indian languages, literature, art, history, better to say, to know Indian culture in its totality and not only its philosophy. Among his direct pupils, now attached to Instituto Italiano peil Medio ed Estremo Oriente Rome (IsMEO), are Prof. L.Petech, Prof. Fillipani Ronconi and Prof. Raniero Gnoli, both great scholars of Sanskrit. Prof. Paolo Daffina, scholar of modern Indian language and literature was sent by Prof. Tucci to Nagpur to study with Prof. Raghubir.

Prof. Maria Spagnoli is an expert of Indian art. Prof. Tucci's other two direct disciples are Prof. Giorgio Renato Franci and Prof. Amalia Pezzali. Prof. Franci is a scholar of Sanskrit and is the director of the Department of Glottology at the University of Bologna. At present he teaches Sanskrit and modern Indian languages. He came to Calcutta on Tucci's advice to study Sanskrit and modern Indian languages. He visited Santiniketan several times in the fifties. Prof. Amalia Pezzali is an eminent scholar of Buddhism. She came to India to obtain a Ph.D in Buddhist philosophy and religion at the University of Benaras under the guidance of eminent philosopher Prof. T.R.V. Murty. She was a professor of religions and philosophies of the Far East for over twenty years at the University of Bologna. She went to Venice on the invitation of Georgio Cini Foundation to open there an oriental section. The Foundation published in four volumes "*Civilta dell a oriente*" (Civilisations of the orientan Encyclopaedic work in four big volumes) general editor of it was Prof. Tucci.

In Turin Prof. Oscar Botto, famous scholar of Sanskrit, a friend of Prof. Tucci, heads the "Cesmeo" (Piedmontine Center for the study of Middle and Extreme Orient). He was confered the degree of D.Litt. Honoris Causa from Benaras Hindu University very recently. In Milan and Florence, there were Tucci's orientalist friends like Prof. Vittorio Pisani and Prof. Belloni Filippi, who wrote an article on Tagore in the Tagore Centenary Volume of the East and West published from ISMEO under the editorship of Prof. Tucci. It is a journal published in English. All these associates of Professor Tucci are well acquainted with the works of Tagore. Some visited Santiniketan several times. They often speak of Tagore and his literature in their class lectures and quote Tagore in several of there articles.

Here I shall discuss about an interesting essay. I was amazed when I came across with an essay of Prof. A.M.

Pizzagalli, a friend of Tucci and of Prof. Benoy Kumar Sarkar, the eminent professor of Sociology at Calcutta University, in a journal of the Institute of Glottology in the University of Bologna. He was inspired by both his friends Tucci and Sarkar to study the major modern Bengali poets. In this essay he discusses the influence of Dante Alighieri, the great mediaeval Italian poet on some Bengali poets of 19th C. An Orientalist recording the influence of an Occidental mediaeval poet on a group of poets of the Orient with a remarkable curiosity. Here is a gist of his articles. He writes that in Calcutta a society called "*Bangiya Dante Sabha*" was formed around 1938 in which the famous personalities of Neo-Indian culture took part, although he does not mention the names.

In 19th Century two of the major Bengali poets had known the works of Dante and drew from the Divine comedy some characters. Madhusudan Dutta in his heroic poem *Meghnād Vadha Kāvya* and Hemachandra in his work *Chhyamayi* takes the theme from Dante's *The Inferno (hell) of the Divine* comedy.

The imitation consists in this, that both the poets describe voyages after death into Hell and they let their hero be guided by two ladies. Madhusudan Dutta makes the hero find on the door an inscription which reminds the lines of Dante (lay down all hope you that go by me - "*Lasciate ogni esperanza di andar fuori*". He mentions a third poet Kumar Sarkar also influenced by Dante, but he writes in English.

In *Meghnād-Vadha Kāvya* Madhusudan writes that the hero Rama visits the world beyond death guided by a lady Maya, an allegorical personification of the illusion of the phenomenal world. The picture of Hell depicted by Dutta resembles that of Dante. Like Dante he meets with the persons known to him when alive and sees the torments and those who are tormented.

But according to Pizzagalli the hell of Madhusudan lacks the solid structure that Dante gives to his hell. The inscription is a reminder of Dantesque Hell. So the points of similarity between Dante and Madhusudan Dutta are three: (1) The journey to the hell, (2) the lady guide, (3) the writings on the door. A fourth one- the meeting with persons known is of less value as the poet might have derived it from some other Indian or Persian epical poems.

The other Bengali poet Hemachandra in his poem entitled "*Chhāyā Mayī*", narrates a visit of a living man guided by a lady to heaven and to hell. The girl Amari guides her hero as Beatrice guides Dante from star to star and from planet to planet and reveals to him the secrets of the world beyond death. The division of sin and the sufferings is a subject of much discussion in the Bengali poem, like that of Dante.

If these poets had known Dante certainly they had known him through English translations. But he does not mention the translations which might have been available to these poets. He then tries to make a comparison between some ideas of Dante and Indian philosophical ideas. The belief in the advent of avatara or divine incarnations. The prophecy of Veltro reminds him of some of the verses of *Bhagavadgitā*, in which Krishna announces the coming of a redemptor of the world. But there is a major difference. The Veltro of Dante is not an incarnation of God as in the *Bhagavadgitā*, he is a mysterious man who would come to save the world.

Two tendencies, one represented by Kumar Sarkar and the other represented by Madhusudan Dutta unite them with Dante. Kumar Sarkar evaluates Dante as a political liberator. He compares him with Mazzini, one of the makers of Italian "Risorgimento". Madhusdan Dutta instead exalts in Dante his mystical aspect and is influenced by it. He does not hesitate when Madhusudan says that Dante for more than fifty years exercises on him an abiding influence. According to him Dante is a greater poet than Virgil as his sentiment of the *Infinite* is sincere and fundamental. The mysticism pervades all his works from *Vita Nuova to Commedia* and it is possible to find in the thoughts of Dante the mystical experiences of Bengali Vaisnavism. Dante, thus appears to the Bengali poet of 19th century as a political agitator of the conscience towards liberty or as a mystic, who revearls in his work - the experiences of the *Infinite.* This is important to Prof. Pizzagalli, to understand the influences of Dante outside Italy. He concludes that the Indian world is perhaps better than that of Islamic in the sense that it is ready for a comprehension of an Italian poet, more for the mystical side than that of political or religious side. The firm Catholic faith of Dante, his Romanity or Latinity would always lay an obstacle in understanding his works outside the Catholic spheres. The Indians would understand and interpret Dante according to their mentality. This is good and it should be like this. The Indians might reveal Prof. Pizzagalli hopes, some new aspect of Dante undiscovered or escaped by the Italians. The experience of the Divine poet would be thus richer and fuller.

Tucci's Scientific Expeditions to Nepal and the Bon Religion

10

Arpita Chatterjee

It is a fact well known that Giuseppe Tucci travelled extensively in Nepal and Tibet in order to study their history and culture. His travels have exposed the fact that a very strong bond exists between the two countries. He realized the importance of a better knowledge of the cultural and political history of Nepal in order to investigate and study the evolution of Tibetan culture. He undertook five journeys to Nepal and in the process found that its history was by no means confined to the valley itself. In fact, the country consisted of innumerable principalities and tribes with different cultures and traditions. With time many of these had developed and peaked off but the outer world was hardly knowledgable about these happenings. Tucci, very rightly thought it essential to visit the interior regions of Nepal specially the country's western and central parts about which practically nothing was known.

With this aim in mind Tucci took a trip in 1952 which was a journey to Gorkha, Pokhra, the Valley of the Kali Gandaki upto Mustang and the Nepal-Tibet border, and on the way back, through Muktinath and Dsarkot down to Baglung, Palpa, Rummindei, and from the last back to Pokhra through Nuwakot.

The two roules followed by Tucci in his expeditions to Nepal

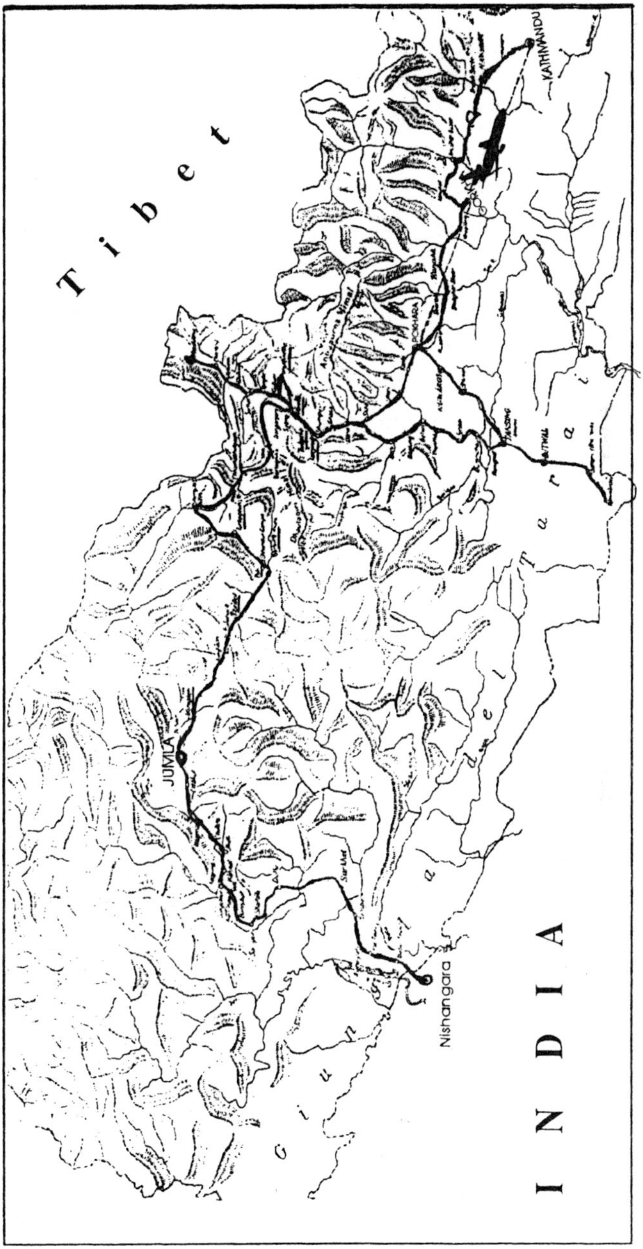

Courtsey: G. Tucci Preliminacy Report on two Expeditions in Nepal

In 1954 he took another trip this time his aim being the valley near Jumla. His route this time was from Pokhra to Tukucha, then after crossing some high passes he went to Charkabhotgaon and Tarapgaon. After investigating these villages he came back to Barbung Khola—Thuli Bheri and through Tibrikot he reached Jumla. From there he proceeded to Chilkha, then to Dullu and finally through Surkhet he reached India at Nishangara.

In course of these trips he collected innumerable important materials which he wrote down in the form of a preliminary report on two scientific expeditions in Nepal. These journeys and the subsequent report is of vital importance for the reconstruction of Nepal's history and culture and his itinerary upto Jumla is also relevant for the materials revealed for the study of Bon and Tibetan Buddhism.

Tibetan Buddhism begins at Larjung which is about two hours walk from Tukucha and Tibetanization increases and becomes more pronounced as one goes northwards towards the Nepal-Tibet border.

Marpha which lies a bit to the north of Tukucha is one of the Bon pockets of Nepal. However, a lama called Samgye zang Po had come to the district from eastern Tibet and was responsible for the revival of Tibetan Buddhism there. He spent a lot of time in Marpha, in the *gompa of ku zug de nga* which is built on a ridge to the north-east of Marpha, in Tukucha and Ge-Kar. It seems, he put an end to the slaughter of animals as a sacrifice as was practised by the followers of the Bon religion. This shows that the people of that area (Thak district) practised their original religion Bon, uninfluenced at that time, or influenced very little by any other religion including Buddhism. Even though *Sam gye zang pos*' exact time cannot be pin pointed, (he was born in the year *sing rta* — wood horse), this must have been inhabited by many pre-Buddhist people like the Bon followers, as the survival of some ancient beliefs and rituals still show.

Tucci found Bonpo communities in Charkha and Tarap, both of which lie to the north west of Marpha. Even a Bonpo manuscript has been found there. This book is composed following the method of the Buddhist tantras, and the various mantras in it are said to hold the essentials of the teachings and the doctrine of the Bon religion. This manuscript contains allusions of *yod pa* and *medpa*, that is the division of this universe into two sides; the good and evil creation respectively. The principal doctrine is the fundamental difference between beings and their painful existence, and the very purpose of the revelation is to come to their rescue.

During Tucci's trip of 1952, he observed certain rituals which he had no hesitation in terming as non-Buddhist or Bon. While referring to what he wrote in the diary of that journey, he said: "On our way back to the camp, we saw a lama on a horse back, coming towards us. He was bearing a puppet, stuffed with green plants that looked like juniper, covered with a green tunic; its face was hidden behind a white mask on which human features were drawn. A five pointed wooden tiara was placed like a crown on its head and each of the five triangular rims was inlaid with the figure of one of the five supreme Buddha's; round its neck hung silver pendants. A young man followed, carrying a kind of tray on which were placed offerings and little branches of burnt juniper. Alongside the man on horseback walked a lama intoning psalms and beating the drum of sorcerers (damaru). Another lama led the horse, holding in his hand a white scarf, the other end of which was tied to the stud's neck. As soon as they reached the river bank, they stripped the puppet off its clothes, pendants and diadem, and threw it in the river with the juniper and the offerings"

These rites confirmed Tucci's opinion on the survival of Bon rites in these districts, the memory of which even Buddhism in its advance had been unable to obliterate. He felt that the rites of both religions superimposed on one another in these places.

The person who had died the day before had been left in the mountains for animals to devour after the body had been cut into pieces. However, straw image was made and it was this that was thrown into the river. This is very much a Bon ritual which Buddhism could not remove and obliterate simply for the practical reason that there never was and there still is very little wood in Tibet which could be spared and used on the dead.

Buddhism in Nepal helped in the spread of Tibetan rituals there, but they were also accompanied by some Bon rituals like the practice of casting the corpse in the river. Instead of abandoning the old beliefs completely the people had compromised by throwing an image of the corpse in place of the corpse into the river.

Again, the white scarf used in Bon rituals in many places including the China border, is the emblem of the rope which in the original form might have been like a bridge, joining the earth to the sky on which the deceased walked up to heaven.

Tucci also found the Bon cult of the hearth among the Thakalis of Tukucha. Even at the time of his writing the sanctum sanctorum of their house was the hearth in the middle of the kitchen. It was protected by a low wall that surrounded it on all sides. On this wall around the hearth, he found jars full of barley kept for the manes of the dead, and a tall brass lamp burning in a corner. No one except family members were allowed to pass beyond a line and violate its sanctity.

The traveller found Bon pockets also in Charkha, Tarap, Pale and a few other places on the way to Jumla. Pale he found to be the meeting place of Buddhism, Hinduism and Bon. After crossing Pale, he found Hinduism ruling unopposed.

In connection with the Bon religion of Nepal, it can be said that its origin lay in pre-Buddhist Tibet. Earliest texts reveal that it was simply referred to as *lha-chos* 'sacred doctrines' and *gnam sai lugs* 'pattern of heaven and earth'. Invokers were called *Bon* and the sacrificers *gshen*. It was only at a later stage when the indigenous religion began to be permeated with Buddhism that the religion began to be called Bon and the followers of the religion as Bonpo. Retrospectively, Bon refers not only to the early indigenous religious practices of pre-Buddhist Tibet but also to the religion that developed in close interaction with Buddhism from the 8th century onwards. This in its turn has caused quite a bit of confusion. In many aspects the Bon religious system of pre-Buddhist Tibet was not only different from Buddhism but also from the Bon religious rites as practiced in later centuries.

This early indigenous religion was mainly preoccupied with the cult of the royal dead and the continuation of life beyond death. Elaborate rituals were performed in order to ensure the safe passage of the deceased to a post-mortem land of bliss. The soul was safely conducted there by an appropriate animal—usually a horse, yak or sheep—and it was usually sacrificed during the funerary rites. Many other offerings also accompanied the dead. These rites reached their heights during the funerals of kings and noblemen.

The royal dead according to these rites was entombed with food, drinks, precious objects and even close companions who were buried alive. Their funeral rites were extremely elaborate, lavish and magnificient. Enormous funerary mounds were created, large numbers of priests and officials performed these rites which often lasted for several years. Later on, this practice of burying alive of companions was humanised a bit, and they were permitted to live at the tomb itself. However, they could not keep any contact with the outer world and other living men and women. The main purpose of these rites was to ensure the happiness of the deceased in the land of the dead and also to obtain their beneficial influence for those living. This indigenous religion does not suggest of another life in heaven or hell and the departed soul belonged essentially to the realm of the dead.

In general this original religion was also primarily concerned with affairs of this life. They took the help of astrological calculations and other means to discover the cause of human misfortunes and then prescribe suitable cures. In fact Bon was a kind of Shamanism with sorcery being one of its principal features. It involved ritualistic worship of spirits and tutelary deities of various kinds. These spirits, local gods, and demons were mostly responsible for all the misfortunes and they were pacified by ransom offerings. In these rites ransom offerings were very common and they included sacrificial victims like human beings, but one does not find proof of this from the historical period — that is the 7th century onwards.

One of the most important and venerated of the indigenous religion is their Lord of the Soil; He is worshipped by means of an upright stick or pole, often decorated with pieces of rag or coloured cloth. Another important cult was that of the local gods who were also very powerful and were conceived as mighty warriors with a host of fighting attendants. Some local gods were also connected with mountains. In fact, legend has it that the first king of Tibet descended from heaven unto the mountain called *yar-lha-sham-po*. In later years, with the advancement of Buddhism, the indigenous religion began to be permeated with the influence of the former and even Buddhism took in a considerable amount of the Bon features in order to strengthen its hold among the Bonpos.

Buddhism gave to Bon the suggestion of yet another life in heaven and hell. Gradually, a new religious order evolved and Bon priests began to incorporate Buddhist doctrines and practices. Temples and monasteries were built on Buddhist patterns and from them the Bonpos developed their own set of philosophical works with changes only in terminology. They formed the Bon tantric rules corresponding to Buddhist tantras both in content and intention. However they centered on Bon divinities. Finally, systems of yoga and meditation were developed in the religion and even treatises and manuals were written on them. It was found that by the 14th century the indigenous Bon religion had evolved into a special kind of Buddhism even though the Bonpos claimed that their teachings did not come from India. Earlier it proposed in western Tibet with its centre being *Sharg-Shung* which corresponds to modern western Tibet with mount Kailash as its centre. In the 7th century A.D. it was absorbed by the expanding Tibetan empire. Originally Bon had come from even further west from the land of *stag-gzigs* (Tadzhig ?) which might be pre-Muslim Persia and *Mi-bo-gshen-rab* who was the founder of this religion also came from there. His biography was, however, shaped on Sakyamunis' biographical model. In their conventional set of doctrines called 'Nine ways of Bon', their earlier teachings were grouped under placating of gods and demons, ransom offerings and prognostics together with stupa worship, practice of ten Buddhist virtues, religious asceticism, tantric rituals and even higher tantric practice of using mystic circles as means of spiritual integration. Finally it also contained the highest level of yoga where all means and methods are transcended. It is recognized as having similarities with the different Buddhist schools in Tibet specially the *rning-ma-pa* sect. Later on, following the *dge-lugs-pa* sect, their teachings emphasised on strictness of monastic life, in the study of philosophy and logic and even in awarding the degree of *dge-bshes* for the skill they, acquired in philosophy and logic. One can safely say that even though Bon has been referred to as Shamanism, only certain limited features can be attributed to the pre-Buddhist indigenous religion, and in its subsequent development it has lost most of its Shamanistic features and has become more or less a special kind of Tibetan Buddhism instead.

Coming back to Nepal we find that the Bon prevalent there is also very much contaminated by Buddhism specially by the *Dsoge cen* and *bka-rgud pa* sects. Both the religions are superimposed on the other and it is difficult to define the limits between the two even though Tucci is of the opinion that this diffusion of Tibetan Buddhism is of recent date. Lamas came here only a few decades ago, made converts and built shrines and monasteries. As a result the local Bon communities inducted many Buddhist doctrines and teachings into their own. There is so much similarity between the two that one who is not well versed with things Tibetan including the language would not be able to realize that the inscriptions on the stones piled up on the *mani* walls are not the usual *om mani padme hum* but the Bon mantras *om ma tri mu ye sa le adu*; *om a dkar sa le od, om yar om od a*. This diffused Bon religion found in remote pockets of Nepal is also an adaptation of the primitive beliefs, rituals, cults and ideas into a scheme of religion which has been influenced a great deal by the advanced religions like Buddhism, Hinduism and others. Tucci prefers to call it the secondary form of Bon.

An example of this secondary Bon is to be found at the small shrine *bsaṃ gling* near Muktinath which was founded by a Bon Lama from Kham. He had to contend with Buddhism which was represented here by the *Sa-skya-pa* and the *rning-ma-pa* sects and later by the *bka rgud pa* sect. Paintings representing some Bon deities are to be found above the door of this shrine. Mantras, formulas and invocation to some gods are found written at the back of these paintings. The text shows that these details belong to the secondary form of Bon and the invocations are similar to those of the rNing-ma-pa sect. As Tucci has said, 'Even their liturgical and dogmatical background is the same as that concerning the *nairātmyajñāna, Upāya and Prajñā, sunyatā etc.*

Along the tracks near Charka and Tarap, Tucci found innumerable *mcod-rten* but as exploration was impossible it could not be said whether they belonged to the Bonpos or the Buddhists.

In Charka the first Bon temple is *Bla ma ni ma* and the track leading upto it runs near the *mani* walls inscribed with Bon mantras. The temple contains the *rnam-tar* of *Mi-bo gsen rab* in its larger redaction along with many images and deities.

Another temple which has no name, but has only *Bon po lha khang* written, has a curious goddess with the image of a deity in her right hand and a vase in the left. Yet another temple is dedicated to *Gu-ru-rin-po-che* but it has in it frescoes representing the Buddhist as well as pure Bon deities. Even though this Bon religion is contaminated by Buddhism, the pure Bon deities are quite old and do not show great similarity with Buddhism. This seems to reveal that the process of Buddhism in the stretch of the country is not very old.

In the Bon temple of Tarap called the *T'ar rgyas pun ts'ogs glin* Tucci found preserved the *rnam tar* of *mi bo gsen rab* in twelve volumes and huge *mcod rtens* with Bon *swastikas* created along the road.

Pale is the last village with a largely Bon population and where Tibetan is spoken and understood widely. The Headman was found to be a follower of the Bon religion but in a temple in Tibrikot he had painted frescoes where *Brahmā, Visnu, Siva and Krsnā* exist side by side with *S'ākyamuni* and the Bon master, *Mi-bo-gsen-rab*. On the way from Pale, Tucci found some *mcod-rten* which looked like gates with the road passing under it. On its ceilings are frescoes represented by Bon deities displayed round the five *Bon-sku*, the centre being *rtog rgyal ye ses mkyen*.

Tucci also found stones erected in the fields which the Bonops beleved to be the shrine of a *lha* or that the *lha* (god) protecting the field finds shelter in these fields itself.

The local Bonpos disposed off the dead by throwing the corpse into the river. However, in some cases the bodies were also burnt and the ashes deposited with a circle of stones being arranged round that place. Along the road before Charka, Tucci did find stones arranged in circles which were burial places for the Bon people.

Tucci found Bon pockets as far as Munigaon on the other side of Morialekh. It is a village inhabited by breeders and traders of ponies called the *Khampas*.

In a country like Nepal, which is predominantly Hindu and to a much smaller percentage Buddhist, it is strange to find pockets where the Bon religion and rituals are still being practised by the people. That too in places which are not in immediate geographical proximity to one another or to the Nepal-Tibet border.

R.L. Turner's comment in his *The People and their Languages* might give an explanation for these pockets still in existence.

"In a population of under six millions, in all there are spoken at least scores of languages, all mutually unintelligible, and some broken up again into numerous and often very different dialects. Even within the limits of a single valley there may be a village, the inhabitants of which speak a language completely unintelligible to their neighbours a mile or two away."

This feature of one language being unintelligible to the other even a mile or two away has been caused mainly by the difficult and harsh topographical conditions of the country which made communication very difficult. It naturally resulted in their local, social, cultural and religious traditions being isolated from one another, while this has helped them in maintaining the purity and uniqueness of their cultural heritage, there has also been a definite lack of interaction between their different cultures including religion. We find that till recently, this indigenous religion based on some sort of shamanism, had very little influence from outside. This was much more applicable in the difficult areas. On the other hand, where communication was easier this religion had been combined with another, and dominated or driven away by the forces of Buddhism and Hinduism. In Nepal these Bon pockets are difficult and isolated places, they were not commercial or trade centres and communication was not easy either. The situation there might have resulted in some people clearly practising their indigenous religion—Bon, while others apparently followed other religions, which were nothing but combinations of the latter with the rites and rituals of the original indigenous Bon religion.

References

1. Giuseppe Tucci, *Preliminary Report on Two Scientific Expeditions in Nepal.*

   Serie Orientale Roma X

2. Materials for the Study of Nepalese History and Culture. Institute Italiano Per Il Medio ed Estremo Oriente, Roma, 1956.

Giuseppe Tucci: His Realm of Archaeological Adventure and Discovery in Trans-himalaya

11

Subrata Chakrabarti

Giuseppe Tucci's four score and, two months less than, ten years of extraordinary life was maked by a single minded cause to the development of archaeology of the Transhimalayan region. For this cause his adventures stretch from the snow-clad inaccessible land of Western Tibet to Iranian Sistan where rain fires. During a long span of his life, Professor Tucci explored for 44 years, wrote for 72 years, contributing research and popular writings since 1911 till 1983. Interestingly Professor Tucci did not share his world view with other notable of his contemporaries such as Frazer, Durkheim, Hertz, Mauss and Malinowski. These scholars tended to see the particular in the general, advocating segmentary ideas or vertical dimension to the society or culture they were concerned with. As against this, Professor Tucci had his own distinction - the horizontal dimension that the East and the West, both classical and modern, was not opposed to each other, as it is usually conceived of, but coalesced with each other to form a complementary and an inseperable concept - Eurasia. As he wrote quite apropos:

> Europe and Asia have since the dawn of history been closely joined and intercommunicating through migration, invasions, conquests, trade, pilgrimages and interchanges of the arts and ideas, so that not one single event of any significance has ever occurred in one part without having reacted on the other, thus establishing the just claim to a common history, a history, that is of Euro-Asian Contitent (Tucci 1958:344).

As an autodidact from university days till to the end of his life, Professor Tucci maintained this stand. To cite an example from another piece of his writings two decades later:

> Europe and its historians have committed a stupendous error in regarding Asia and Europe as two distinct continents, while in reality they ought to speak of a single one, Eurasia, so conjoined in their parts that no remarkable event in one has not had its reflex in the other (Tucci 1977a).

Elsewhere Prof. Tucci did more emphatically say: to set forth the undoubted evidence for what I have been saying, and to induce scholars to renew our writing of history and, why not, to dampen the fire of our European arrogance, which is so slow to die (Tucci 1977b).

Professor Tucci's realm of archaeological adventure in the East and his interest in language and culture of Greece and Rome will have to be evaluated with this Tuccian position in the unity and diffusion of culture. With this quest of unity as he 'entered the labyrinth of Orientology', Professor Tucci also turned to archaeclogy.

This chapter attempts to highlight the significance of the lesser talked about subject of pre-and-pro-historic archaeology of Transhimalaya of which Professor Tucci gave a succinct summary, and guidelines for future research as well. These are described below under the following heads:

1. Expedition in Tibet 1929-1948
2. Pre-and-proto-history in Tibet

3. Cave Archaeology in Tibet, and
4. Megalithic Archaeology in Tibet

Expeditions in Tibet (1929-1948)

The travellers, few in number, who have found way to Tibet, writes Tucci (1973:13), have almost always been concerned to describe the customs of the country or have been mainly interested in geographical, sociological or religious research. Even those who have studied the culture history of Tibet have mostly neglected the archaeological aspects of their subjects and devoted their attention to questions of more strickly religious or liturgical interest. Giuseppe Tucci deliberately depated from this research and he himself has emphasised: In my own travels in Tibet I concerntrated on its archaeology and the history of art (Tucci 1973:13).

By archaeology he even meant pre-and-protohistoric archaeology and whatever data he could collect have been faithfully reported.

Pre-and proto-history in Tibet

The archaeology of human origins in Tibet is still speculative and no research attempt worth the name uptil now has been directed to achieve this objective. Perhaps the attempt to draw up a programme to fill this void goes to Professor Tucci. He not only planned but sought to excavate a cave at Luk in Western Tibet (Tucci 1973). However his programme of excavating the cave was frustrated as the hostility of the village people was too evident towards the Luk cave excavation which Professor Tucci was obliged to abandon no sooner than he began excavting. Thus bring back the palaeolithic archaeology of Tibet to square one: in beginnings came end.

The Neolithic archaeology in Tibet due to absence of exact point of reference is also sketchy but not so conspicuous by absence of objects as that of the Palaeolithic stages.

In the course of his travels in Tibet, Tucci has reported to have come across a fair number of objects known in Tibet as *thokde (t'ogrdeu*, "stone fallen from the sky") or *thoding* (*mt'o Idin*, high flying) i.e. thunder stones. Later a chance discovery of a skeleton near Nyelam (Ne lam), between Tibet and Nepal, in association with ground stone implements is not only historically significant but also help pushed back the antiquity of man in Tibet to the Neolithic Period (Erh-Chien 1972 cf. Tucci 1973: 33).

Cave Archaeology in Tibet

Tucci also has drawn the attention of scholars to numerous caves in Tibet, some of which on the basis of recovered objects could be dated to the 2nd millennium B.C. , if not earlier. In addition to the Luk cave already mentioned, Tucci has referred to other caves in the Nubra area and the caves in Kun Lun (de Terra 1940), at Lhaste, Yandogtsho (Waddell 1905), Janthang, Yarlung, Dotakdsong. In addition three caves Tsapang, Chang (P'yan) and Khyunglung (K'yun Lun) from western Tibet also find mention in his account of Tibetan cave sites.

True that the archaeology of the caves in Tibet is still in a state of limbo as there is no excavation at any of these caves but in some sites, as at Tsapang, Chang and Khyunglung, the caves were used as dwellings only in winter, since in summer the whole population would move to high plateaux with their flocks and herds, returning to the caves when the cold weather came on (Tucci 1973). This is not unique to Tibet alone, it is equally true to an inhabitated rock-shelter near Ghaligai in Swat where archaeological excavation (Stacul 1967, 1969) have proved that they were occupied by man since upper palaeolithic time. Citing such example, Professor Tucci, infact, argued strongly for Tibet that at least in some, if not all caves, archaeological probing might establish such a contunity of culture.

Megalithic Archaeology in Tibet

The Megalithic archaeology in Tibet is not as frustrating as that of her preceeding stages of culture. The evidence for this is though not stupendous but convincing.

Megaliths in Tibet are described by Tucci as 'large stones set in the ground, either by themselves or in group, arranged in circles or sometimes in square formations or in alignments. In the middle of the group there may be either one or three taller stones set erect in pilasters, left in their natural state without any dressing'. Such sites have been reported form Pu (sPu), on the frontiers of Tibet as well as in the mountains about Shapgeding (Sab dge sdins) and on the road between Doptadsong and Sakya. In addition, Tucci has also reported monolithic stelae as megalithic tombs on the plateau leading to Zhidekar (gZi sde mk ' ar) in Western Tibet, at Byi'u near Lake Manasarovar, and, in the regions bordering on Tibet, at Garbyang and Doptakdsong (Tucci 1937, 1973).

While classifying the megalithic tombs and shrines of Tibet, he has grouped them in two categories: cult sites and burial grounds and concluded that a distinction must be made between circular or square structures with a central pillar or *doring* (rdo rin) and those without a central pillar (Tucci 1973). Furthermore, analogy has also been drawn on the basis of objects made on copper, bronze and, even, iron and setting of stones in the megalithic tombs and shrines to the other parts of Tibet and Mongolia (Bacot 1909, Bacot et al 1940) and Kokonor region (Stein 1957). Reference has also been made to the tombs found in Swat and the Indus Valley (Stacul 1967, 1969). However, the chronology of these tombs and shrines are yet to be ascertained. Nevertheless on the basis of all these evidences, it has been suggested (Hummel 1958) that there existed in Tibet a megalithic proto culture developed out of neolithic tradition which moved along two routes: one leading through the corridor of the Euro-Asiatic steppe in the Kokonor region into central Tibet and perhaps extended into Tsang, the other running into Kashmir and Spiti (Hummel 1958). Professor Tucci (1973: 57-58) did not disapprove such a broad based hypothesis but cautioned against any firm conclusion as the materials so far obtained from Transhimalaya are from unexcavated sites, notably graves.

To conclude it is in graveyard that we find Professor Tucci's interest lay as an archaeologist for whether in Swat or Iranian Sistan what one can notice that he always made his first attempt to locate graveyard, 'because' to quote him 'graves are dark, silent books which, however, through various signs left for the future investigator, can speak to us of a past which is perhaps not yet dead (Tucci 1977 b: 22).

Foundation in the dust of humanity is a universal percept that Professor Tucci did tend to highlight in all his archaeological mission. It is not in isolation that man and his culture flourish. In his study of archaeology and culture of Transhimalaya, the central point too is this unity. As he himself has aptly exclaimed that the Tibet is not an island cut off from the rest of the world but a meeting place of different cultures, an area in which Indian, the Himalayan regions, China, Iran and Central Asia all exert their various influence (Tucci 1973). As a great explorer Professor Giuseppe Tucci left for posterity a huge blue print, translating them into reality is the responsibility of those to whom he left behind with a sound advice:

> The time has come to teach history in another way-no longer the history of Europe (or, still worse, of the West, because the West can be anywhere in our Planet, depending on the point we are looking from), but the history of the Eurasian Continent (Tucci 1977 b:17).

Bibliography

Bacot, J. (1909); *Dans les marches ṭibetaines.* Paris

Bacot, J., F.W. Thomas and C.Toussaint. (1940); *Documents de Touenhousang relatifs a' 1 historie du Tibet.* Paris

DeTerra, H (1940), *Durch Urwelten am Indus*, Leipzig.

Hummel, S. (1958), *Der Ursprung des Tibetischen Mandalas*, Ethnos p.158 ff.

Stacul, G. (1967), Excavation in a Rock Shelter near Ghaligai (Swat, West Pakistan): Preliminary Report, *East and West,* 17:185 ff.

Stacul, G. (1969), Excavations near Ghaligal (1968) and the Chronological Sequence of Protohistoric Cultures in the Swat Valley (West Pakistan), *East and West* 19:44 ff.

Stein, R.A. (1957), Les k' iang des marches sino-tibetaines, *Annuaire de l' Ecole Pratique des Hautes Etudes 1957-58*, Section des Religions, p.4. Paris.

Tucci, G. (1937), *Santi e briganti nel Tibet ignoto,* Milan. (revised by the author in 1978 and reprinted with the title *Tibet ignoto*, Rome: New Compton).

Tucci, G. (1948), Preistoria Tibetan *Rivista di Antropologia* 36: 265-268.

Tucci, G (1958), Considerations of an Historian: A Propos (Sic) East and West, *East and West* 8: 343-349.

Tucci, G. (1973), *Transhimalaya, Archaeologia Mvndi Series,* Geneva: Nagel Publishers.

Tucci, G. (1977a), New Areas of Research for Archaeologists and Buddhologists, *Journal of the International Assocation of Buddhist Studies* 1:71-74.

Tucci,G. (ed.) (1977b), La Citta, *Bruclata Del Deserto Salato/The Burnt City in the Salt Desert.* Venezia: Erizzo Editrice.

Waddell, L. (1905), *Lhasa and its Mysteries,* London.

A Study on the Mahāyānavimśikā of Ācārya Nāgārjuna

12

Narendra Kumar Dash

The *Mahāyānavimśikā (Mahāyānavimśikā:* Bhattacharya) of Ācārya Nāgārjuna is a fundamental work on the Mādhyamika philosophy. This small work, (Tibetan[1]:21; Tibetan:23; Chinese:24, and 28 in Sanskrit), for the first time, was edited by S. Yamaguchi and published in the *Eastern Buddhist*, Vol. IV with its English translation. Having gone through this edition of Yamaguchi, Bhattacharya reconstructed the lost Sanskrit text from the Tibetan and Chinese versions of the same text. There are two Tibetan translations of the said text.[2] The first one was translated into Tibetan by the Indian Pandit Chandrakumāra and Bhiksu Sākyaprabha *(Tib. Dgo-slon sā-kya-od)* and the other text was translated by the Indian Pandit Jayānanda and Bhiksu Kirttibhutiprajñā *(Tib. Dgoslon grags-byor-ses)*. There is no mention that these translators knew about the other translation. Besides, there is a Chinese translation of the Mahāyānavimsikā.[3] This Chinese translation was consulted by Yamaguchi and Bhattacharya for their editions of the text. It is known from the colophon that the Chinese translation was done by Dānapāla (shehu).

Again, in 1956, Prof. Tucci edited the text. He, however, consulted the Sanskrit manuscript of *Sāradā* scripts. According to Prof. Tucci the work was preserved in the Cor monastery. Tucci mentions that the Sanskrit text was compiled in between 8-9 century A.D.[4] The Sanaskrit text does not follow closely either the Tibetan versions or Chinese one. Our study on the mentioned works of the same text suggests that not only the arrangement is different but some of the lines of the Sanskrit work are not at all found in the Tibetan and Chinese versions. Here it may not be out of context to mention that the Tibetan and the Chinese versions agree with each other and they have a close agreement regarding the number of stanzas. On the other hand, the Sanskrit text has more verses, at least seven in number.

Arrangement

The Tibetan and Chinese versions of the text *Mahāyānavimsikā* begin with a benedictory verse. Bhattacharya reconstructs the verse as:

> *namo vācā 'vācyamapi dayayā yena desitam /*
> *dhīmate vītarāgāya buddhāyācintyasaktaye // T. V. 1*

It means: "salute to Buddha who is wise, free from all attachment, and whose powers are beyond conception and who has kindly taught the truth which cannot be expressed by mere words". This opening verse of the Tibetan and Chinese versions has been inserted in the middle of the Sanskrit text as the eighth one. On the other hand, the Sanskrit text opens with the following verse:

> *na jñācchūnyatā nāma kācid anyā hi vidyate /*
> *viviktāvyatirekitvam vivekasya yato matam // S. V. 1*

Prof. Tucci translates the verse into English as: "There is no void as something different from knowledge, in so far as it is known that a discriminating judgement implies nonexclusion of the notion discriminated."[5] Now this opening verse of the Sanskrit text needs some study. The 3rd and 4th *pādas* of the verse seems to be taken from another text. In the *Abhisamayālaṅkārāloka* of Haribhadra, which is a commentary on the *Prajñāpāramitās*, we have the following lines on the verse seventeen; viz., ...*viviktāvyatirekitvam vivekasya yato matam' iti nyāyāt tadvyatireko' pi pṛthak lokottarena mārgena prāpyate na tu kriyate ityaktrimārthena* (p.25). This seems to be exactly taken by the compiler of the Sanskrit verses of the *Mahāyānavimśikā*.

Again, verses four and five of the text, which have been edited by Prof. Tucci are identical with two verses of the *Laūkāvatāra-sūtra* we have the following verses:

> *cittamātre nirābhāse vihārā buddhabhūmi ca* /
> *etadhi bhāṣitam buddhairabhāsante bhāsayanti ca* //4.1
> *cittam hi bhūmayah sapta nirābhāsā tvihāṣṭamī* /5
> *dve hi bhūmī vihāro'tra se sā bhūmirmamātmikā* //4.2

These two verse are also again found in the tenth chapter of the *Laṅkāvatāra-sūtra*. Here the stages of *citta* and the *cittabhūmis* have been described. I would like to give the English translation of the said two verses here: "Mind the imageless (8th stage), the dwellings (9th, 10th stages), and the Buddha stage (11th stage): this has been said by the Buddhas; this they are saying at present, this they will say". "Seven stages are mere mind, the eight stage is the imageless. The following two are dwelling there, the remaining one is made of myself". Again, the next two verses of the *Mahāyānavimsikā,* edited by Tucci, are also meant for the description of the cittabhūmis and the stages of the Bodhisattvas. According to these two verses seven stages of the cittabhūmi have been preached by the Buddhas as being subject to mind and in the seventh no depravity of mind, word and body evolves. Because all sorts of notions regarding the character of things are removed (*sarvabhāvasvabhāvalaksana vyudāsāt; Laṅkāvatāra-sūtra*). In the eight stage, even dream, its support (depravity's support), is not the cause of pleasant feelings. Thus, in these two verses, the cittabhūmis and the stages of the Boddhisattvas are being described. These two verses are also found in the *Laṅkāvatāra-sūtra.*[6] Thus we may conclude that the four verses, i.e. four to seven, have been taken from the *Laṅkāvatāra-sūtra* by the compiler and these were not originally composed by the author of the *Mahāyānavimśikā*. The subject matter of these four verses are also seems to be out of context here. Our observation is further supported with the fact that the verses discussed above are not found in the text reconstructed by Bhattacharya on the basis of the Tibetan and Chinese versions.

Now, we would like to say something about two verses those found in both i.e. in the Sanskrit text, edited by Tucci, and also in the text reconstructed by Bhattacharya.

The first verse is:

yathā citrakaro rūpam yaksasyātibhayan karam /
samālikhya svayam bhītah samsāre'pyabudhastathā //

(T¹. V.10)

It means: "just as a Painter is frightened by the terrific image of a demon which he himself has painted, so the fool is afraid of the samsāra, which is created by his ignorance". Prof. Tucci has rightly pointed out that the said verse has been taken from the *Kāsyapaparivarta*?[7] The latter, which is the concluding verse of both texts (i.e. the Sanskrit text and the Sanskrit reconstruction) has been composed only for the glorification of the *Mahāyāna* viz.,

kalpanājalapūranasya samsārasumahodadheh /
anākramya mahāyānam ko vā pāram tarisyati //

(T². V. 22)

Bhattacharya, while reconstructing this verse, prefers to use the word *gamisyati* instead of *tarisyati* of the Sanskrit text. In the Tibetan version we find the word' *byuū-bar-'gyur*. According to my opinion the word used by Bhattacharya seems to be more appropriate here as the previous word *pāram* and the present word tarisyati (tr) possesses almost an identical sense. The same verse as it is with a single variation (*Vajra* in the place of *Mahā*) is also appears in the Jūānasiddhi of Indrabhuti.

Bhattacharya opines that "this identity is not accidental but is a deliberate quotation by Indrabhuti from the *Mahāyānavimśikā*".[8] This opinion of Bhattacharya is not supported by Tucci. He argues that "the very verse has not been inserted in the Jñānasiddhi from the *Mahāyānavimśikā*, but rather added to the text of *Mahāyānavimsikā* at a latter time, only as a glorification of the *mahāyāna*". He again says that this "seems to be justified here by the fact that if the last verse will be eliminated, the title *Mahāyānavimśikā* becomes justified with exactly twenty verses".[9] This remark of Tucci losses the ground. He identifies the author of the text with the great philosopher Nāgārjuna, who flourished in the later half of 1st century A.D. or first half of 2nd century A.D. On the other hand, Indrabhuti, the author of the Jūānasiddhi is believed to have flourished in the 7th century A.D.[10]

Thus, on the basis of our study, we conclude that at least nine verses from other texts have been interested in the Sanskrit text of the *Mahāyānavimśikā*.

Title: Now, we would like to say some words on the title of the work. The title *Mahāyānavimśikā* is a compound word. It has two components i.e. *Mahāyāna* and *Vimśikā*. The literal sense of the the former word is "Great vehicle". After the death of *Buddha*, his disciples, direct or indirect, differed in interpreting his teachings. This is evident among others from the facts of the councils and the formation of a number of schools, everyone of which claimed to be the true expounder. To this is to be added the evolution of a number of *mārgas* 'ways' called in the system *yāna* 'vehicle'. In this context author of the *Sarvadaranasamgraha* says that it is true that the master taught his disciples the same thing, but owing to their varied dispositions they understood it differently.[11] Thus, though there are different *yānas*, in fact, there is not more than one *Yāna*. There is not end of *Yānas*, so long as the consciousness or mind (Citta) remains in motion (Pravartate), but when it turns back there is neither a *Yāna*, nor one who goes thereby. In the *Laṅkāvatāra-sūtra* it has been said that "I say difference if difference of *yānas*, but this is only for the purpose of attracting the ignorant people viz.,

Yāna vyavasthā naivāsti yānamekam vadāmyaham/
parikar ṣānārtham bālānām yānabhedam vadāmyaham//[12]

Though there are different *yānas*, still the highest truth (*paramārthasatya*) is to be obtained from the *Mahāyāna* and the *yānas* are like the staircase lead one to Mahāyāna viz.

ādikramikasattvasya paramārthāvatāraṇe/
upāyastvyam sambuddhaih sopānamiva nirmi tah//[13]

In the *Mahāyānasūtralaṅkāra* it has been said that the Mahāyāna is the best way (vehicle) of the *Buddha dharma* i.e. *dharmasyottamayāna*...etc.[14] Thus Asaṅga uses the word *uttamayāna* 'best vehicle' in the place of *Mahāyāna* 'great vehicle'. Again the Hinayanists are self-centred and individualistic. They want their individual salvation and their equipment is inferior. The Mahayanists are intent upon acquiring enormous quantum of merit, not for their own benefit, but to achieve the salvation of all persons of lower or mediocre endowment. They are not selfish. They make free gift of their spiritual wealth to those who are lagging and have not the energy to achieve their own welfare. The Bodhisattva is the ideal being who has taken upon himself the task of saving all sinners. Until the last creature is saved, the Bodhisattva will not think of his own salivation. Therefore, *Mahāyāna* named as *Bodhisattv yāna*. Lastly, Asaūga cites a verse which clearly shows the differences between Ūrāvakyāna (Hīnayāna) and Mahāyāna (Bodhisattvayāna) viz.,

āsayasyopadesasya prayogasya virodhatah /
upasthambhasya kālasya yat hinam hīnameva tat // [15] *1.10*

In this verse *Hīnayāna* has been condemned as very narrow because of its five points of difference with the *Mahāyāna*. These are firstly, the narrow aim of self-liberation and, secondly, the narrow teachings to realise that aim, thirdly, the narrow method applied for this realisation, fourthly, insufficiently of equipment and, fifthly, the shortness of time within which final liberation is guaranted (verse 10). In fact, the *Mahāyāna* school is always characterised by a broadness of outlook, and deep sympathy for the suffering beings and thus, it is termed *Mahāyāna*.

Again, S.B. Dasgupta suggests that the word *Mahāyāna*, as we find it mentioned in the 'Awakening of faith in Mahāyāna' (*Mahāyānasraddhotpādasūtra*) of Asvaghosa, meant the highest principle or reality, or the knowledge which is the primordial source of the universe as a whole; and all the objects, animate and inanimate, are nothing but the manifestations of that one unchanging and immutable principle, and only through it, final salvation of all beings is possible. But historically *Mahāyāna* refers to the school of Buddhism which is styled by its adherents to be the great way salvation because of the universality and generosity of its tenets (vide; *An Introduction to Tantric Buddhism*; 1950; pp. 5-6).

The word Vimsikā can be understood as—where we find twenty verses. Thus, the word vimsika signifies that it very small (kshudra) in nature. Bhattacharya, however, says vimsaka.

The title vimsikā shows that it is a book where we get twenty verses. However, we think, both the word are correct grammatically. Thus, the whole word *Mahāyāna-vimsikā* means—a work with twenty verses which explains the fundamental features of the *Mahāyāna* system.

Author : It has been stated in the colophon of the text that Årya Nāgārjuna is the author of the work under discussion.[16] It is known from the history of Buddhism that there were at least three Nāgārjunas of different times. In the colophon nothing has been mentioned that to which Nāgārjuna the present work is affiliated. Bhattacharya, in his introduction to the *Mahāyāna-vimsikā*, has doubt that whether the work is composed by the philosopher Nāgārjuna, who was the founder of the *Mādhyamika* philosophy and who flourished in 1st or 2nd century A.D. The second Nāgārjuna, to whom Bhattacharya affiliates the present work, was born in the 7th century A.D.[17] Besides, there was another Nāgārjuna, an alchemist, perhaps contemporary to the second Nāgārjuna. Prof. Tucci, however, opines that the author of the text under discussion, is the philosopher Nāgārjuna (1st Nāgārjuna). After a long discussion he remarks that "the conclusion, therefore, seems to be that while there is no solid argument for denying that the vimsikā was written by Mādhyamika teacher and no stylistic reasons prevent us from supporting definitely his relationship of this treatise".[18] This view of Tucci is not supported by Winternitz. He is of opinion that the Mahāyāna-vimsikā is affiliated to the second Nāgārjuna, who flourished in the seventh century A.D. This is also supported by two other famous scholars of modern times i.e. K. Venkatraman[19] and H. Nakamura[20]. Again, from the Tibetan account, we however, do not get any reference about the second or third Nāgārjuna. Thus, the authorship of the present work is a controversial issue. We are not sure that to whom the work is actually affiliated. We have also not sufficient proof in this matter. But we can safely presume that the work was composed at least one hundred years before 8th century A.D., as its first Tibetan translation was made in that time. This also does not solve our problem of authorship.

Date: Earlier, it has been mentioned that our text was translated into Tibetan, for the first time, by Chandrakumāra and Bhiksu Sākyaprabha. Bhattacharya says that these two translators were contemporary of Gopala, the founder of the famous Pal dynasty of Bengal in 8th century A.D. Again, since Nāgārjuna is the author of the work, it cannot be composed later than the last part of 7th century A.D. Thus, the work was definitely composed before or during the 7th century A.D.

Now, the question arises that whether the Tibetan translation of the work was made on the basis of the Sanskrit original or on the basis of the Chinese translation. This question does not exist as the Chinese translation was made only in the 10th century A.D. by Dānapāla, Dānapāla was flourished in the later Sung dynasty (960-1127 A.D.). Bagchi, in this connection, says that "in 982 the emperor appointed a board of translation at the head of which were place in three Indian scholars *Fa-t'ien* (Dharmapāla), T'ien-si-tsni and She-hu (*Dharmapāla*). It was probably due to their activity that the Chinese Buddhist collection was enriched by 201 volumes between 982 and 1011".[21] On the basis of this observation of Bagchi, Dharmapāla, perhaps, had translated our text in 10th and early 11th century A.D. Then, now we may conclude that the first Tibetan translation was made directly from the Sanskrit original.

Subject Matter

In the opening verse the author wants to give his homage to Lord Buddha who is wise, free from all attachment, whose powers are beyond conception, and who has kindly taught the truth which cannot be expressed by words. It is a general practice that at the beginning of the work, our ancient author should pray to their respective Lords or Goddesses to complete the work without any obstacle. Therefore, Pataūjali has rightly said that :

māūgalika ācārya mahatah sāstraughasya maūgalartham siddhasabdamāditah prayuūkte /

maūgalādini hi sāstrāni prathante virapurusakāni ca bhavanti āyusmatpurusani ca, adhyetārasca siddhartha yathā syuh iti //.[22]

According to Nāgārjuna, there is no origination (*utpādah*) and also there is no destruction (*nirodhah*) in the transdental truth. Just as in dreams one experiences different objects in different places and countries without there being any objective existence of them, there is nothing generates and nothing destroys in this world, all appearances are but transformations of the principal of consciousness by its inherent movement. This is also the main point of the Vedānta philosophy. Thus, the theme of Vedānta philosophy is surprisingly similar to the idealism of Nāgārjuna as taught in his *Mahāyānavimśikā*. Again, he says Lord Buddha is like the sky which has neither origination nor cessation and the creatures also possess the nature of Buddha. Thus, there is no birth either on this the other side of the world. The karmic forces (*samskārah*) originate as dependent on conditions; but they are not born out of an essence of their own. Therefore, it is void (*sūnya*) by its nature. This fact will never be cognised by ordinary and ignorant people, but this fact comes into the range of knowledge of an omniscient one. All the things are regarded as reflections by nature. They are pure and *sānta*, devoid of any duality, equal and remain always and in all circumstances in the same way (tathatā). The ignorants think there is a self (*ātman*) where there is no self. Like that they imagine happiness, misery, indifference, passions and liberation viz.;

asatya ātmani cātmatvam kalpayitvā prthag janāh/
sukhad uhkham abhijūāsca sarvam esām ca tattvatah// S.12

Actually birth in the six realms of existence, highest happiness in the heaven and the great pain in the hell, do not come within the perview of truth. So also the notions that unmeritorious deeds lead to the extreme misery, old age, disease, and death and the meritorious actions surely bring good result. As a painter is frightened by the terrible figure of a *Yaksa* which he himself has drawn, so is a fool frightened in the world by his own false notions. A fool falls in a mud which he himself prepared, in the same way beings are drowned in the mud of false representation difficult to cross over. Looking at what is non-existen as if it were existent, they experience a painful sensation, equally all objects of experience which are false harrass them with the poison of doubt.

Seeing beings so helpless the Buddhas whose mind is steady in compassion and intent on the benefit of others enjoin them to the pursuit of illumination, because they desire that the beings also, having accumulated the necessary accumulations and having obtained the supreme knowledge, freed from the bondage of false notions (*kalpanājāla*), may become one day Buddhas, the friend of world viz.;

te'pi sambhrtasambhārāh prāpya jūānam anuttaram/
kalpanājālanirmuktā buddhāsyurlokabāndhavah// S.20

He who realizes the transcendental truth knowing the *pratityasamutpāda* on the manifestation of entities depending on their causes and conditions, knows the world to be *sūnya* and devoid of beginning, middle or end. For them, there is neither a *samsāra* nor a *nirvāna*, and these two are mere appearances; the truth is stainless, changeless, and quiescent from the beginning and illumined. The object of knowledge in dream is not seen when one awakes. Similarly the world disappears to him who is awakened from the darkness of ignorance. Therefore, there is nothing which can be regarded as a real thing such is the nature of all things.

One having origination (jāti) does not originate himself. Origination is a false conception of the people. Such conception and conceived beings, these two are not reasonable. All this is nothing but mind (*citta*) and exists just like an illusion. Hence originate good and evil actions and from them good and devil birth viz.

cittamātramidam sarvam māyākāravad utthitam/
tatah subhāsubham karma tato janmah sūbhāsubham//

When the wheel of the mind is suppressed, all things are suppressed. Therefore, all things are devoid of *ātman* or independent nature, and consequently they are pure viz.,

sarve dharmā nirudhyante cittacakranirodhatah/
anātmānas tato dharmā visuddhās tata eva ca//

Though there is nothing eternal, still fools think the things which have no independent nature as eternal. They also think about a self, a pleasure in things which are in fact unsubstantial. Thus, the ocean of existence (*bhava*) appears to one who is enveloped by the darkness of attachment and ignorance. Lastly, Nāgārjuna says that knowing the truth, that which is taught in the Mahāyāna, one can reach the other side of the great ocean of sansara, which is full of water of false notions. Again, the false notions do not arise in a man who thoroughly knows this world.

This is the theme of the Mahāyānavimsikā of Nāgārjuna.

References

1. Mdo Tsa Folios 166[a].4—157[a].5; Cordier Vol. III, p. 293 and Pek. 5233. Mde ga° Folios 211[b].B—213[a].2; Cordier Vol. III, p. 357 and Pek. 5465.

2. Refer; B. Nanjio No. 1308 viz, *T a-shan-rh-shi-sun-lun*. The Chinese title may be reconstructed into Sanskrit on: *Mahayanagathavimasti* sastra. According to Nanjio the very work was composed by Bodhisattva Nagarjuna and the work agree with Tibetan K'-yuen-lu.

3. Refer; Tucci, G; *Minor Buddhist Texts*, pt.1. p.195.

4. *Ibid*; p.204

5. cf; The *Lankavatarasutra*, edited by Vaidya, P.L; reproduced from Darbhanga, p.87.

6. *Ibid*; Verses 104 and 105.

7. Refer; *Thei Kasyapaparivarta*, p.100.

8. Refer; *The Introduction to the Mahayanavimsika*, ed. by Bhattacharya, V; Calcutta; 1931; p.5.

9. Refer; Tucci, G; *The Minor Buddhist Texts*, pt.1. p.199.

10. Refer, Bhattacharya, V; 1931; p.4.

11. cf; *yadyapi bhagavanbuddha eka eva bodhayita tatha—pi boddhavyanam buddhibhedaccaturvidhyam/. The Sarvadarsanasamgraha, p. 35.*

12. The *Laūkāvatāra-sūtra*; verse No. 2/203 and 10/445. In 2/203, we have the word *Yānabhedam* in the place of Yānamekam, which seems to be wrong.

13. The *Tattvaratnavali* of Advayavajra, p. 21 vide; Bhattacharya, V; *The Basic Conception of Buddhism*, University of Calcutta; 1934; p. 32.

14. The *Mahayanasutralankara* of Asanga, ed. by Bagchi, S., Darbhanga; 1970; p.1.

15. *Ibid*; p.4. It has been said in the commentary on the above verse that: *sravakayane hyatmaparinivanayi-vasayastadarthamevopadesastadarthameva prayogah paritasca punyajnanasambharasamgrhita upastambhah, kalena calpena tadarthapraptiryavattribhirapi janmabhib/ mahayana tu sarvam vipryayena/ tasmadanoyavirodhad yad yanam hinam hinameva tat// na tanmahayanam bhavitumarhati/ Ibid: p.4.*

16. Refer; *Mahayanavimsika krtir aryanagarjunapadnam;* The Minor Buddhist Texts, pt.1. p.203.

17. Refer; *The Introduction to the Mahayanavimsika,* ed. by Bhattacharya, V; 1931; p.4.

18. Ref; Tucci, G; *Minor Buddhist Texts*, pt.1. p.200.

19. Refer Vekata Ramanan, K.; *Nagarjuna's Philosopy*, Delhi, 1993; p.34.

20. Nakmura, H; *Indian Buddhism* (A Survey with Bibliographical notes), Delhi; 1989; p.241.

21. Bagchi, P.C.; *India and China*; Bombay 1951; p.55-56.

22. Refer; The *Mahabhasya* of Patanjali (*Paspashnnika*). Beside, the Bhasaparicheda of Bisvanatha Bhattacharya has a detail study on the justification of the *mangatacaranam* at the beginning of a work.

Reflections on Professor G.Tucci's Remarks on Madhyānta-Vibhāgaṭīkā and Abhisamayalaṃkāra

13

Rita Gupta

One of Professor G.Tucci's greatest contributions to Indological studies lies in his restoration of some Yogācāra Sanskrit texts from Tibetan translations, and tracing some Yogācāra Sanskrit texts form Nepal and Tibet. Two such texts restored and edited by Professor Tucci are *Madhyānta-Vibhāga (Vibhaṃga)- tika* and *Abhisamayālaṃkara*. The main *kārikās* of these texts are by Maitreyanatha, and the commentaries (*ṭīkās*) upon them are by Sthiramati and Haribhadra. Professor Tucci wrote a monograph (by way of an introduction to the contribution of Maitreyanātha), entitled, *On Some Aspects of the Doctrines cf Maitreya (nātha) and Asaṃga.* Besides introducing briefly the contents of *Madhyānta-Vibhāga-ṭīkā and Abhisamayalaṃkāra*, this monograph also contains some observations of Tucci on some basic doctrines of Maitreyanatha. I would like to present before the readers a critical survey of Tucci's account of: (i) the contents of these texts and (ii) the basic doctrines of Maitreyanatha, as Tucci thinks, are reflected therein.

(1) I would like to start with *Abhisamayalaṃkāra*. Mahāyāna and early Buddhist literature seem to have taken some apparently divergent views on ontology, religious ideals and practices. Out of the numerous examples of these divergences, mention may specially by made of Mahāyāna concepts of : (i) emptiness of *dharmas*, (ii) identity of *saṃsāra* and *Nirvāṇa*, (iii) the three *kāyas* of Buddha, (iv) the *bodhisattva* ideal and (v) the ten different planes of meditation. These concepts do not seem to fit in, easily, with the early Buddhist onto-ethical and spiritual framework. Mahāyānists, accordingly, attempt a reconciliation of these divergences by making a distinction between the literal and the intended meanings- the *nitārtha* and the *neyārtha*. The distinction implies that the typical Mahayānist conceptions are the results of probing deeply into the apparent literal meanings. The *neyārtha* in the Mahayānist opinion, is ultimately derivable from the *Buddha-vacanas*, preached, on different occasions, in accordance with the moral and intellectual abilities of the various creatures to whom they are expounded.

The fact remains that it was certainly difficult to combine, in a coherent way, all practical, metaphysical and theological aspects of the Mahāyāna and early Buddhist schools. The challenging task of making a consistent correlation was attempted by Maitreyanātha in *Abhisamayalaṃkāra*, where the so-called 'Hīnayāna' and 'Mahāyāna' *caryā* or religiosity are combined in, what Maitreyanatha calls '*abhisamaya*', that is, mystical ascension, through meditation, towards the supreme realization.

By the completion of his training and the accumulation of his merit (*punya-sambhāra*), the *bodhisattva* enters the path of intuitive illumination (*darśana-mārga*), and that of concentrated meditation (*bhāvanā-mārga*).

The higher reaches or planes of the meditational path are traced, with a wealth of detail, and an intimate account of the intuitive experiences encountered in those planes, in *Abhisamaya* and its *alamkara* by Asamga. The *alaṃkāra* is not a commentary in the usual sense of the term, inasmuchas it does not explain any particular passage taken singly. On the contrary, it explains a body of Mahayana *sūtras* taken as a whole. One of its aims is to support the Mahāyānist claim that the Mahāyānist special conceptions, such as those mentioned earlier are not epicryphal interpolations. They are, rather, new ideas concealed in the venerable texts.

The ideal of *bodhisattva* is a special Mahāyāna contribution to Buddhist spirituality. The early Buddhist schools placed supreme importance on individual liberation of the *sādhaka* known differently as *śrāvakas* and *pratyeka buddhas*, the Mahāyānists opine that the *śrāvakas* (who attain *Nirvāna* by listening to the preachings of the *arhats*) are always busy with their own salvation. They have no concern for others who are suffering. The *pratyeka-buddhas*, who do not require any instruction of teachers, are bent on their own liberation through leading a solitary life of self-control. By contrast, the Mahāyānist extols the virtues of *bodhisattvas*, who are not bent on attaining enlightenment for themselves. They dedicate their lives for the service of others, and they try to help others to attain *Nirvāṇa*. They are equipped with *prajñā* or intuitive wisdom of *śūnyatā* of *dharmas* and universal compassion (*mahā-karuṇā*) for the suffering unenlightened people.

The *bodhisattva* undertakes the preparatory discipline for attaining *bodhi* (*bodhicittotpada*). The chief characteristic of a *bodhicitta* is its immeasurable wisdom of *śūnyatā*, unfathomable *mahā-karuṇā* and its limitless *upāya-kauśalya*. Realisation of *śūnyatā* culminates in *prajñā*, intuition of: (i) the noumenon or *Nirvāna*, and (ii) essencelessness and realitivity of the phenomena or *saṃsāra*. *Śūnyatā* is identical with *Tathatā* or the Absolute. This *prajñā* leads to the realization, on the part of the *bodhisattva*, of his identity with all others, resulting in the endless compassion for other suffering beings. As a result of this compassion the *bodhisattva* develops the skill in adopting any expendiency whatsoever for the removal of their suffering and bondage of those beings. The *bodhisattva* is required to make certain resolves including the one that he would remain in this world and not embrace *Nirvāṇa* till others have been helped to do so. One of his resolves would take the following form: let my unlimited knowledge, compassion and expediency (*prajñopāya*) be of unending service to beings. Being fully enlightened, let me make efforts to induce other beings to take the Mahāyāna path of supreme enlightenment. All this is summed up in the commentary of *Abhisamaya: śūnyatā-karuna-garbha-bodhicitta-samutpādya samyaksambuddho bhūtvā yathā-bhavyatayā parārthaṃ prati triyāna-dharma-deśanādibhir-yatnam kuryāmīti praṇidhānaṃ krtvā pratipattyā sampadayediti".*

After the production of the *bodhicitta* the adept becomes a *bodhisattva* and proceeds to an upward ascension through ten different stages or *bhūmis*, starting with *arcismati* and ending with the *dharmamegha* (when he becomes Buddha or fully enlightened). In these ten stages the *bodhisattva* practices the ten perfections known as the *pāramitās*: *dāna* (charity), *śīla* (good-conduct), *kṣānti* (forbearance) *vīrya* (energy), *dhyāna* (meditation), *prajñā* (intuition), *upāya* (expediency), *praṇidhi* (concentration), *bala* (strength) and *jñāna* (wisdom).

The conception of the *practice* of the ten *pāramitās* reflects an attempt to reconcile: (i) the Mahāyānist and early Buddhist paths to attain spirituality, and (ii) the specific Mahāyāna ideal of spirituality as exemplified in the *bodhisattva* ideal, vis-a-vis the early Buddhist ideal as expressed in the *arhat* ideal.

Early Buddhist spiritual discipline incorporates the threefold structure of *śīla* (moral practice), *samādhi* (concentration) and *prajñā* (wisdom). The *Mahāyāna pāramitā* doctrine modified and elaborated this structure in the tenfold *paramitā*-discipline of: *dāna* (*charity*), *śīla* (moral practice), *kṣānti* (forbearance), *vīrya* (energy), *upāya* (expediency), *praṇidhi* (concentration), *bala* (strength) and *jñāna* (knowledge).

Several *Mahāyāna* texts developed the *pāramitā* doctrine. They are: *Pancavimśati-sāhasrika-prajñā-pāramita, Aṣṭasāhasrika-prajñā-pāramitā, Prajñā-pāramitā-hrdaya-sūtra. Mahaprajñā-pāramitā-śastra, Abhisamayalamkara* is supposed to be commentary on the *Asta sāharikā prajñā-pāramitā.*

The *Mahāyāna pāramitā* doctrine revolutionizes the early Buddhist conception of the *pāramitās. Dāna, śīla, kṣānti, dhyāna*, are not, in the *Mahāyāna* context, seen as disconnected acts. They have only one aim to make a man fit for the highest knowledge. A mind swayed by passion and attachments cannot perceive the truth. Practice of *dāna, śīla and kṣānti* lifts the mind above such sways. All the other *pāramitās* are meant to purify the mind in such a way that it can receive the intuition (*prajñā*) of Śunyatā. *Prajñā-pāramitā* alone can complete the other *pāramitās*; can make each of them a *pāramitā*.

Abhisamayālaṃkāra discusses, under eight heads, the process of meditation of the *sādhaka,* form the preparatory moments upto the final stage. The fundamental moments of this process are represented by *trisarvajñatā*, viz. the *sarvajñatā* or omniscience of the *śrāvakas* and *pratyekabuddhas*, the *margajñatā* or omniscience of the path of spirituality of the 'Hinayanists' and 'Mahayanists', and *sarvākārajñatā* or complete wisdom which is supposed to correspond to Buddhahood. The latter represents the final goal of the spiritual process.

It is pointed out by Tucci, in his remarks concerning meditation, as enunciated in *Abhisamayālaṃkara*, that the world-stuff, which displays itself before the meditator's mind in the process of meditation, is not ultimately real. The object which projects itself is nothing else but the moment of our consciousness. The progress of meditation towards the *sarvākārajñatā* of the ultimate stage is *realised* through a successive series of moments, which are nothing but supports of the immediately following ones. This instantaneous support or *ākāra* develops in our mind from mind itself, without any relation to an independent object. Everything is true in the very moment in which it is thought. But it will not be so in the next moment, when a *sādhaka* progress, a new *ākāra* will take as the place of the former one. And it will be a mistake to have any attachment (*abhiniveśa*) to the former.

In Tucci's opinion, the idealistic tendencies, which are developed in a more systematic way by the followers of Maitreya, have been foreshadowed in the frame of the mystic ascension of the *sādhaka*.

(2) Let us now pass on to the first book, *Madhyāntavibhamga* or *Madhyāntavibhāga*. The predominant theme of this work is an elucidation of the metaphysical aspects of the Yogācāra system. The use of the term, '*Madhyantavibhāga*' is significant here, as it connotes the difference of the position of this work from that held by *Mādhyamikakārikā* or *Madhyamakakārikā* of *Nāgārjuna*.

Tucci remarks that, according to Nagarjuna, the 'middle position' or '*madhyamā-pratipad*', consists in neither negation nor affirmation. *Dharmas* or ultimate existents, according to Nāgārjuna, are neither existent nor non-existent, because they are *śūnya*. What Tucci actually means here is that, according to Nāgārjuna, things which are dependently originated (*pratīya-samutpanna*) are *śūnya* (empty) of essences (*svabhāva*). Hence they are not real existents. Nor are they non-existent, inasmuch as they are grounded on reality (or *Nirvāṇa*) as their substratum. Tucci adds that, according to

Nāgārjuna, *Sūnyatā* itself cannot be said to be affirmative existence, inasmuch as any affirmation is the effect of construction (*vikalpa*). And I may add, that, that which is imaginative construction (*vikalpa*), distorts the vision of reality. Tucci makes some obscure remarks at this point. "*Śūnya* is therefore the consequence of *prasaṃga*, but it cannot become a *graha*, because it would then be a *dṛṣṭi*." By *prasaṃga* is obviously meant here the *reductio ad absurdum* argument and a kind of dialectical reasoning. But what Tucci means here by "śūnya is therefore the consequence of *prasaṃga*" is far from clear. He perhaps means by it the fact that realisation of *Śūnyatā* (not *śūnya*) or *Tathatā* is attained through emptying the mind of all imaginative construction, by a dialectical reasoning. But, then, the possibility that *Śūnyatā* itself is regarded by Nāgārjuna as a noumenon (as opposed to phenomena) is completely ignored by Tucci in his remark.

For Maitreya, Tucci remarks, things stand in a different way from that conceived by the *Mādhyamika* philosophers. *Śūnyatā*, according to Maitreya, becomes the *dharmatā*; and this *dharmata* is *sat* or existent insofar as it represents the *ens realisimum* of the *dharmas*. But this *Śūnyata* is also *asat* or non-existent, insofar as it consists in the privation of duality (*dvaya), grāhya and grāhaka*, object and subject, which is always inherent in the contingent experience. This *Śūnyatā* is, in Yogācāra, another name for pure consciousness (*vijñapti-mātratā*). Following Sthiramati, the commentator of *Madhyantavibhaṃga*, Tucci says that *Śūnyatā* is real and unreal at the same time. This point, Tucci adds, is summarized by Maitreya in the following *kārikā*:

> "*Abhutaparikalpo' sti, dvayam tatra na vidyate;*
> *śūnyatā vidyate tatra, tasyām sāpi vidyate*".

Tucci translates the *kārikā* as : "The unreal imagination is; duality does not exist in it. But the voidness exists in it, and it also (viz, the unreal imagination) exists in this (voidness)".

The first stanza of the *kārikā*, Tucci says, is meant to refute the extremist point of view of those Buddhists who denied existence of a *dharma (sarvadharmānam śūnyatā)*. This extreme point of view or *anta* can hardly be considered as a right doctrine. If everything is *śūnya*, the *Yogācāra* contends, it would in fact be impossible to strive after liberation. Therefore, he says, the *abhūtaparikalpa* is (*asti*). Here *abhūtaparikalpa* consists in the wrong assumption of the objects which are not self-existent.

(A) Tucci goes on to say: these *abhūtaparikalpas* are represented by an endless series of mental states which have no beginning, but will end with *Nirvāna*, and are said to correspond to the process of *saṃsāra*. They are related to one another in a relation of cause and effect, and extend to past, present and future.

(BI) But this *abhūtaparikalpa*, Tucci continues, is in fact devoid of any content (though it appears as containing subject-object duality). There is no perceiver or perceived in it. It is also a condition of pure existence devoid of any qualification. Therefore, *Śūnyatā* exists in the *abhūtaparikalpa* inasmuchas it is devoid of subject-object dichotomy-*grāhya-grāhaka-rahitam vastumātram.*

Tucci pointed out that the above *kārikā* is intended to refute the theory which does not admit the existence of voidness (but, at the same time, wants to maintain the possibility of removal of *avidyā* and *kleśa*). The reasoning contained in the above is as follows:

If we were not to admit the existence of *Śūnyatā*, there would be no support to meditation, so that it would be impossible to undertake the spiritual discipline leading to liberation.

It is important to note here that if Tucci is referring here to the theory of the Mādhyamika, then he is not giving an adequate representation of the latter's philosophy.

Madhyamikas represent the ultimate reality or *Tathatā* as *Śūnyatā*, in the sense that it is devoid of, or transcends, the *vikalpas* or conceptual constructions of: ***ens, non-ens***, both *ens* and *non-ens*, neither ***ens nor non-ens***. Yet, to arsert that it transcends conceptual construction is not to assert that it is nothingness. Moreover, Mādhyamikas do advocate a form of spirituality to attain *Nirvāna*. We take it that Tucci is here merely referring to the Mādhyamika theory as represented in Maitreyanātha's Yogācāra idealism.

If this *Śūnyatā* or ultimate reality, Tucci urges, be existent, and be present in the very *abhūtaparikalpa*, the necessary implicaion is that *mokṣa* is at hand, so that it can be attained by anybody without any effort. We must bear it in mind Tucci is here referring to the common *Mahāyāna* doctrine of the identity of *saṃsāra* and *Nirvāṇa*. *Nirvāṇa* is the ultimate nature (essence) of phenomenal being. But it has to be realised (and not attained) by the removal of *kleśas* (and *avidyā*) which cover the consciousness of the worlding (*pṛthakjana*).

Tucci adds that the *abhūtaparikalpa* or wrong ideation, according to *Maitreya,* resides in *Śūnyatā*. The intended meaning of the remark is: Sunyata is covered and defiled by the *abhūtaparikalpa*. So, it is evident that *Śūnyatā* is just covered, and not non-existent. It must be realized through spiritual endeavour as described in the other treatises of Maitreya.

It is my belief that, as a result of his extreme abbreviation of Maitraya's doctrine, Tucci is lead to misrepresent some doctrines of the latter.

Tucci's conception of *abhūtapaikalpa* is, for example, somewhat misleading. Some of Tucci's remarks about *abhūtaparikalpa* are also, in my opinion, applicable to the *Yogācāra* concepts of *paratantra* and *pariniṣpanna*. And, both *paratantra* and *pariniṣpanna* are, in a sense, different from *abhūtaparikalpa*. To elucidate my point I shall explain below all the three conceptions as I understand them:

(BII) *Parikalpita*: is that which has no authentic existence, but is only imagined. It is an object projected by creative consciousness. This includes whatever confronts consciousness as an other to it, i.e. the external object and the internal ideas, percepts, images.

(C) *Paratantra*: is consciousness as diversified into the various forms. It is called *paratantra*, inasmuch as it is dependent on causes and conditions. Causality operates here on the subjective side. An idea is produced, not by any external cause, but by a previous idea. *Paratantra* includes the whole of phenomenal reality.

(D) *Pariṇiṣpanna*: When *paratanatra* (the subjective) is purified of false duality imposed upon it by the *parikalpita* (the constructed object) it becomes the *pariṇispanna. (ya abhūtaparikalpasya dvayarahitatā sa pariṇiṣpannasva-bhāvaḥ)*" : when the idea of the 'other' (*parikalpita*) is eradicated out of the subject (*paratantra*) it reverts back to its natural quiescence.

According to Yogācāra, no ultimate distinction can be drawn between the *pariṇiṣpanna* and the *paratantra*. The *parinispanna* becomes the *paratantra* due to the infection of the *parikalpita*. The subjective aspect of experience, however, is real, and requires to be purified of objectivity by spiritual *sādhanā*. This purified state is the real nature of the *paratantra* and is identical with it. This is a different version of the Mahāyāna identity of *saṃsāra* and *Nirvāṇa* referred to earlier. Once the false idea of the object is got rid of, the *paratantra* completely lapses into the *pariṇiṣpanna*, the Absolute. So the *paratantra* cannot be held to be different from the *pariṇiṣ panna*, the Absolute. Nor is it completely identical with the former.

From the above discussion it is obvious that some of the remarks Tucci made about the *abhūtaparikalpa* marked by (A) in our writing above, are misleading. The remarks made under (A) are really applicable to the *paratantra*, as discussed in our text, earlier, under (C). It is in the sphere of the *paratantra*, the phenomenal reality, that causality operates. Again, some of the remarks made by Tucci, about the *abhūtaparikalpa*, marked, in our earlier discussion, under (BI), really apply to the *parinṇiṣpanna*, discussed under (D) in the earlier part of the text. According to the Yogācāra, *pariṇiṣpanna* is the absolute, devoid of the subject-object duality. It is pure existence devoid of the states of the *grāhya* and the *grāhaka*.

This confusion, on the part of Tucci, is explicable with reference to the fact, that, Tucci, ignored the point that the concept of the *abhūtaparikalpa* is invented by the Yogācāra Buddhists to emphasize the identity of the phenomena and the absolute (*Tathatā-Sūnyatā*). In order to established their identity- thesis the *Yogācārins* require a common concept that is applicable to both the *paratantra* and the *pariṇiṣpanna*. And *abhūtaparikalpa* is the concept which captures the meaning of both the *pariṇiṣpanna*, the *absolute*, and the *paratantra*, the phenomena.

Abhūtaparikalpa is the Absolute, inasmuch as *Śūnyatā* i.e. the negation of the subject-object duality (entailed by the sublation of the objectivity), pertains to it. It is again phenomena, because the *abhūtaparikalpa,* construction of the false, defiles this *Śūnyatā*-the complete vacuity of the suject-object dichotomy. If the emphasis is laid upon the *parikalpa*, the creativity of consciousness, then it is phenomena, the *paratantra*. But this creative construction is of *abhūta*, of what does not exist. And the creative construction 'the *pariṇiṣpanna*' cannot belong to consciousness in its pristine form 'the *pariṇiṣpanna*'. Thus, if the emphasis is laid upon this pristine form, then the *abhūtaparikalpa* is the absolute.

It is in the light of the doctrine of the identity of the absolute and the phenomena that we are to understand the *kārikā* referred to earlier alleging that *Śūnyatā* (i.e. the vacuity of duality) exists (*vidyate*) in the *abhutapatikalpa (tatra)*. And even unreal imagination (*abhūtaparikalpa*) (*sā*) also (*api*) exists (*vidyate*) in Śūnyatā (*tasyām*) - the absolute devoid of duality.

We have noted earlier that Tucci did not pay enough attention to the subtleties of Mādhyamika doctrines, and this resulted in his somewhat inadequate representation of the latter. This observation can be substantiated by the observation. Tucci's comparison of the positions of Nāgārjuna and Maitreya on p.34 of his book. "But for Maitreya two things exist-wrong ideation as well as *Śūnyatā*. *Nagarjuna* does not say that *śūnya* is *sat*, but, which is rather different, that all *dharmas* are *śūnya*, void. For Nāgārjuna the voidness of *dharmas* has chiefly a logical significance. For Maitreya it acquires an ontological value." The observation of Tucci that *Śūnyatā* for Nāgārjuna has only a logical significance, and no ontological one, is really misleading. Although Nāgārjuna does emphasize the role of *prasaṃga* or dialectical reasoning, his doctrine does not end there. The dialectic of Nāgārjuna is only an end to realise the supreme, the *Śūnyatā*, the *Tathatā*. *Śūnyatā* does have both axiological and ontological significance. The Absolute (*Tathatā*) in Nāgājuna's system is the *paramārtha* which is devoid (*śūnya*) of extremes of conceptualisation: existence, non-existence, both and neither. By a series of sublation of *vikalpas*, with the *prasaṃga* dialectic, the *sādhaka* empties the mind of all hinderances to realisation of the ultimate truth, which is variously termed as *Śūnyatā, Tathatā, Paramārtha*.

By remarking that Tucci was inattentive to the subtleties of Nāgārjuna's thought we do not thereby, in any way, want to undermine the value of Tucci's pioneering works in the field of Mahāyānistic studies. Tucci's writings were confined to the materials available in the nineteen thirties. Many more valuable

Mahāyāna works have, since then, been unearthed, restored and studied by scholars. Were this vast corpus of later discoveries available at Tucci's time, his writings could have overcome the lacunae in his hypothesis. Tucci's contribution lies in his pioneering work which introduced, the scholars of Buddhism, for the first time, to some significant Mahāyānist texts that were not available in Sanskrit in India in Tucci's time.

Bibliography

Abhisamayālṃkara, with introduction and translation from original text, Edward Conze (Series Orientale, Roma, VI, 1954).

Abhisamyālaṃkarāloka of Haibhadra (being a commentary on the *Abhisamayālaṃkāra* of *Maitreyanātha* and the *Aṣṭasāhasrika prajñāpāramita*, ed. with introduction and indices, Giuseppe Tucci, Oriental Institute, Baroda, 1932).

The Central Philosophy of Buddhism, T.R.V.Murti, George Allen and Unwin, Second Edition, 1960.

Madhyānta-vibhaṃga, Translation from Sanskrit, by Th. Stcherbatsky, Indian Studies, Past and Present, Reprint, 1971.

On Some Aspects of the Doctrines of Maitereya (nātha) and Asaṃga, Giuseppe Tucci, University of Calcutta, 1930.

Chinese and Tibetan Materials for Indological Studies 14

(As explored by Professor Giuseppe Tucci)

Suniti Kumar Pathak

A few words regarding the relevance of Tibetan studies in the field of Indological researches may not be out of place here. Indological studies do not mean to know about whats and hows of the history of India and her people. Broadly speaking, Indology refers to study about multifarious traits of the culture belonging to the people of Bhāratavarsa or the Indian peninsula.

The culture traits of the Indian people (Bharata-jana-krsti) have originated and developed in contact with the people residing in the neighbouring countries of Bhāratavarsa. Since the olden days many peoples of Asia and Europe came in touch of the inhabitants of the peninsula.[1] Such as, the Sh'aka-jana, the Kusana, the Bhautta, the Pishāca, the Yona, the Parasika, the Mran or Suvarana-bhūmika, and the islanders of South-East Asia. Apart from the ethnical and trade relationship of the Indians with their neighbouring countrymen, the Indian wisdom did spread outside the boundaries of Bhāratavarsa.

The scope of Indological studies therefore extentds in multi-dimensional prongs. No culture-growth in respect of an individual or a group becomes unilateral. Tibetan studies in that respect are relevant to explore many tenets of the Indian cultural heritage.

On the other hand, the Bhautta peoples of Tibet possess a distinct culture-trait in spite of their topographical remoteness and seclusion. Tibet holds a strategical importance to be in touch of her neighbouring countries surrounding the land like Stagjik (Iran). Gyagā (*Bharata-varsa*), Gyanā (China), Hor (Western Central Asia), Sogyul (Mongolia), the Lalo (West Asia), etc. Tibetan Studies also divert to many thrust areas with references to :

(i) Indo-Tibetan Studies,
(ii) Sino-Tibetan Studies,
(iii) Central Asian Studies,
(iv) Tibeto-Mongol Studies,
(v) The Bonpo Studies to (Stagjik and around), in addition to indigenous culture-traits of the inhabitants of Tibet.

Giuseppe Tucci, one of the leading western scholars in Tibetan studies of our century achieved his grand success by his strenuous efforts together with the Roman spirit of adventure. Professor Tucci followed the foot track of the Italian missionaries who had entered into the remote areas of the Orient for the last three centuries. Prior to them, Marco Polo (1235-1324) journeyed from his native city of Venice upto the Chinese Royal Court by dint of his arduous zeal and inquisitiveness.

Giuseppe Tucci visited Visva-Bharati, Santiniketan in the twenties of our century with no less zeal and inquisitiveness than that his Italian predecessors had. What did inspire Giuseppe Tucci to visit Santiniketan? At Santiniketan Rabindra Nath Tagore, a poet with his vision took a vow to build a seat where the East and the West would meet. He thus wrote in a letter dated November 17,1920.

"When I left you to start for Europe I was labouring under the delusion that my mission was to build Indian university in which Indian cultures would be represented in all their variety. But when I came to the Continental Europe and fully realised that I had been accepted by the Western people as one of themselves, I realised that my mission was of themselves, I realised that my mission was the mission of the present age — it was to make meeting of the call of Santiniketan was invitation of India to the rest of the world. A picture needs its background or its meaning and many people must have its background of larger humanity".

With such vision Visva-Bharati was founded.

Sylvain Levi had come to Santiniketan as the first visiting professor immediately after the inception of Visva-Bharati. He took particular care in initiating broad based researches in the field of Buddhism through the comparative estimate of the materials preserved in Chinese and Tibetan with those in Sanskrit, Pali or Prakrit original.

Professor Tucci had a similar outlook and, with his like-mindedness, he preferred to join Visva-Bharati. In his recollections of Tagore (published in East and West, June-September 1961) he stated thus: "It is, therefore, necessary that Man constructs something durable, that is, find a point of understanding with other men rather than focus his attention on the discords which separate them. Men are evil but Man is good. Only cultural contacts can install understanding and tolerance which reinforce human solidarity because politics and interests dig voids of hate. The good that western culture has done in Asia has been cancelled by merchants and politicians. To the recognition of a benefit has succeeded suspicion or rancour.

Thus, Santiniketan was born, and then Visva-Bharati, ideal meeting of Asia and Europe, destined to restore that balance between reason and fantasy, theory and imagination without which spiritual and intellectual disorder rule in the world. Which is already a mission"

On the above background an attempt is made here to estimate the contributions of Professor Giuseppe Tucci in Indological studies with reference to the Chinese and Tibetan materials. A select bibliography of his academic works is appended.

In Visva-Bharati, Professor Tucci, who was popularly named Tucci-saheb, got an impetus in associating with Pt. Vidhusekhar Bhattacharya Shastri (Shastri-mashay) and other colleagues researcheres on Indology assembled there. An enthusiasm in reconstruction of the Sanskrit Buddhist texts which had been lost in original generated among those researchers of Buddhism as explored from more reading materials in Chinese and Tibetan translations. Professor Tucci also joined the team with a sprit of experimentation.

Meanwhile, the *Mahāyāna-Vimsika*[2] ascribed to Nāgārjuna (?) was reconstructed from its Chinese and Tibetan renderings by Pt. Vidhusekhar Bhattacharya Shastri. Professor Tucci also edited *Madhyānta-vibhāga-sūtra* in collaboration with Pt. Vidhusekhar Bhattacharya Shastri.[3] Subsequently its commentary by Sthiramati, *Madhyānta-vibhāga-sūtra bhāsya tīkā* was edited and published by Pt Shastri.

Pt. Vidhusekhar Bhattacharya was a stalwart in the Indian logic and epistemology and he innovated a trend among his associates. Professor Tucci had also a bend in the field of Buddhist logical critique. Professor Tucci's works on Āryadeva, Ishvarasena, Dingnāga, Asangga,[4] Vasubandhu and Haribhadra Suri were highly admired. The modality of his researches was always to utilise all possible resources available in Sanskrit, Chinese and Tibetan for comparison. His study on Āryadeva's *Catuhshataka* from Chinese sources came out in 1920 and 1925 respectively.

Pre-Dingnāga Buddhist texts on logic from Chinese sources (1929) delineates the analytical perspective of Professor Giuseppe Tucci about the logical treatment of the *anātman* theory on the basis of *pratītya-samutpāda* (dependent origination) which is contrary to the Upanasadic concept of *ātman* and *satkāryavāda*.[5] There were three phases of logical growth in the Buddhist thought:

(i) Pluralistic analysis of *pudgala-shunyatā* tending to *anicca* and *anatta* with reference to the extreme viewpoint of the *Abhidhammika* and the *Sarvāstivāda* outlook (*drsti*).

(ii) Monistic approach towards *sarva-dharmashunyatā* as explained by the exponents of Mādhyamika Nāgārjuna leading to Āryadeva and subsequent *Prasangika* Candrakirti and *Svātantrika* Bhavya or Bhavaviveka.[6]

(iii) *Vijnyānavada* outlook (*drsti*) is established upon the logical critique of *vāhyārtha shunyatā* belonging to two different formulae enunciated by the Buddhist teachers: e.g. (a) *āgamānusārī* analysis by Asaūga, Vasubandhu, Jinendrabuddhi, (b) *nyāyanusari* analysis by Dingnāga, Ishwarasena and Dharmakirti.

In this connection the *Hetutattvopadesha* (Toh. Cat. 4261) ascribed to Jetāri which was reconstructed by Durga Charan Chattopadhyaya during his stay at Santiniketan and was published by Calcutta University 1938, the said text was again published by Professor Tucci (1958) after its find in original manuscripts during his expeditions to Tibet (1948). Prefessor Tucci thus endeavoured to throw a critical perspective on the Indian Buddhist logical method of *hetu* and its subsequent growth in China and Tibet. In addition to that which had been discussed by Stcherbatsky and Satish Chandra Vidyabhusana, a new light was thrown by Tucci.

Giuseppe Tucci also preferred to explore contemporary source materials. He had been in India in the first occasion for about seven years (1924-1931). He then prepared to visit Tibet in 1933 and moved vigorously in spite of his physical strain and hardship. He accumulated plenty of research materials and those came out in his monumental publication in seven volumes of *Indo-Tibetica*.

Tibetan scholars in the West explored a new vista of Tibetan researches which had no longer been restricted to the Tibetan manuscripts, wood-blocked xylographs of the Indian Buddhist texts in translations. The indigenous collected works *gsung'bum* texts got more preference to expose the cross-cultural perspective.

Apart from the literary works in Tibetan, the artistic contributions of the inhabitants of Tibet and those of the Buddhist Himalayas were not ignored by Tucci, as his *Tibetan Painted Scrolls* represent.

In addition to that, the Tantra studies attracted Giusppe Tucci from its applied excellence with inherent symbolism and esoteric interpretations. Tucci had led intensive and scientific expeditions inside Nepal. He could witness the living faith of *Vajrayāna* among the lay-people in Nepal. His works on mediaeval Nepal becomes a source book for Indological studies in the ethno-cultural context.

As the reward of his continuous academic pursuits Giuseppe Tucci was regarded as *the leading authority* of Tibetan studies of his time. His contributions were devoted more on intellectual enterprise to unearth the culture-base of the hetrogenous inhabitants of Tibet and their relationship with peoples of neighbouring countries.

He searched for the ethnic distinction and collected *Tibetan Folk Songs from district Gyantse* and those appeared as the supplementary volume (No. VII) of Artibus Asia in 1949. In the Serie Orientale Roma his work entitled *The Tombs of the Tibetan Kings* with an appendix containing inscriptions and edicts in Tibetan opened a new field of Tibetan studies in 1950. Tibetan studies were no longer the religo-based endeavours with the literary approaches of the Tibetans. Those folk manners in Tibetan culture-growth were presented before the international academicians and social anthropologists.

In this regard Folk religion of Tibet, a section of the *Religions of Tibet* by Giuseppe Tucci deserves mention. The Instituto Italiano per il Medio ed Estremo Oriente (IsMEO) in Rome has been established with an objective in exploring the Orientalia having in the socio-scientific outlook. In 1957 its important publication, *Le Symbloisme Cosmique des Monuments Religions,* which appeared the collection of papers presented in the International Conference held in IsMEO in collaboration of Musie Guimet, may be regarded as milestone in this field. Giuseppe Tucci contributed his erudition in the article on *Symbolism of Bsam Yas temple (It tempio di Bsam yas)*.

It may not be exaggerated to remark that Professor Tucci was an institution by himself. He was the President of IsMEO for decades and also the Director in publication of Serie Orientale cum the Editor of East and West. Many academicians of the East and the West have associated in researches under his academic leadership. Among them, A.Soper, Antonio Gargano, Lucanio Petech, J.F. Rock, R. Gnoli, A Ferrari, T. Wylie deserve mention. The academic activities under the guidance of Professor Tucci achieved excellence when A Bilingual Greeco-Aramaic edict by Asoka published from IsMEO. The monumental work was jointly edited by G. Pugliese-Carratelli and G.Levi Della Vida in 1955 with a foreword by Giuseppe Tucci and introduction by U.Scerrato.

The contributions of Professor Tucci thus become the source of inspiration for Indological researchers. Among them his masterpices the *Tibetan Painted Scrolls* in three volumes may be a guide book for many generations to come in future.

References

1. Chattopadhyaya, Sudhakar: *Racial Affinities of Early North-Indian Tribes* (Munshiram Manoharlal, 1973) p.103 ff.

2. Visva-Bharati Publication, 1924; also, Yamaguchi Susuma (*Eastern Buddhist,* Vol. IV, Kyoto, Japan).

3. Visva-Bharati Annual Report (1929) refers to Maitreya (*nātha*?) as its author. Its Sanskrit manuscript was collected form Nepal.

4. Stcherbatsry, Th.: *The Conception of Buddhist Nirvana*, Laningrad 1924. *The Buddhist Logic* of the same author be also referred.

5. Vidyabhusana, Satish Chandra: *History of Indian Logic*, Calcutta, 1921.

6. Hastings, James: *Encyclopaedia of Ethics and Religion,* Vol. XI, Takakusu, p.198 ff; Levi Sylvain, Toung Pao VII, 1907 p.144f; Dutt Nalinaksha, *Early History of the Spread of Buddhism and Buddhist Schools,* p.271.

APPENDIX

Select Works of Professor Giuseppe Tucci

(A) Buddhism and Indic-Tibetan Studies

(1923) Comparitive Study of Catuhshataka from Hsuan Tsuangs Chinese translation and Sanskrit (Rivista degli Studi Orientalio Vol. X p.521ff, Rome.)

(1923) Studi Lankāvatāra (Rivista degli Studi Origentalio p.567ff, Rome.)

(1923) Saptaśatikā Prajnyāpāramitā (ed) Memorie della R. Academia Nazionali dei Lineci Vol. XVII, Roma)

(1925) On Āryadeva (*Studi Mahayanici: Casa Editrici Italiana*, Roma pp. 521-550)

(1925) Catuhsataka (Italian tran., text and commentary) from Chinese (*Studie Muteriali de stopia delle reliogioni*)

(1925) Bodhicaryāvatāra (Italian tran., Torine)

(1926) Aryadeva's works (Nanjio 1259, 1260) *in Chinese* (T'oung pao, 2 Serie, Vol. XXUV p.16 ff)

(1928) Pre-Dingnāga Buddhist Logic (*Indian Historical Quarterly,* p.550 ff)

(1928) Vādavidhi: it authorship (*Indian Historical Quarterly* Vol. IV, p.630 ff.)

(1929) Pre-Dingnaga Buddhist texts on Logic from Chinese sources (*Gaekowad Oriental Series* XIIX, Baroda).

(1930) *On Some Aspects of the Doctrines of Maitreya—(nātha)* and Asanga, Calcutta.

(1931) A Fragament of the Pratītya-Samutapada Commentary (*Journal of Royal Asiatic Society*; London).

(B) Tantra Studies

(1930) A Sanskrit Biography of the Siddhas (*Journal of Asiatic Society of Bengal*, New Series, XXVI, 138 ff).

(1930) An image of a Devī discovered in Swat (*Journal of Asiatic Society of Europe,* XXVI, p. 120ff).

(1961) *The Theory and Practice of the Maṇḍala* (London).

(C) Works on Tibetan Studies

(1933) Secrets of Tibet (in collaboration with Capt. E. Ghersi tr. from Italian vide the Chronicle of the Tucci's Scientific Expeditions to Western Tibet, 1933).

(1947) The Validity of Tibetan Historical Traditions, India Antiqua, Leiden, pp.309-22.

(1949) *Tibetan Painted Scrolls*, 3 vols, Rome.

(1950) *The Tombs of the Tibetan Kings*, Rome.

(1955) The Scared Character of the Kings of Ancient Tibet, *East and West*, Vol.6, no. 3, pp.197-205.

(1956) The Symbolism of the Temples of Bsam-yas, *East and West*, Vol. 6, no. 4, pp.279-81.

(1956) *To Lhasa and Beyond*, Rome. (Diary of the expedition on Tibet in 1948).

(1962) The Wives of Sron btsan sgam po, *Oriente Estremus*, Vol. 9, pp.121-30.

(1963) The Tibetan White Sun-Moon and Congnate Deities (*East & West*, Sept. pp.133-145).

(1932) Catuhstava (*Journal of the Asiatic Society of Bengal*, New Series, XXVI, p.309ff.

(1932) *Abhisamayālaūkārāloka* of Haribhadra.

(1932) *Madhyāntavibhāga-sūtra* (ed. in collaboration with Vidhusekhara Bhattacharya Shastri.

(1932-41) *Indo-Tibetica*, 7 volumes (Rome) referring to art, literature, iconography, architechture of Western Tibet and Himalayas.

(1956) *Minor Buddhist Texts*, Part I, IsMEO (Istitute Italiano per il Medio ed Estreme Oriente, Roma).

Section 1 The Triśatikāyāḥ Prajñāpāramitāyāḥ kārikāsaptatiḥ by Asaṅga with Introduction.

Appendix 1 Comparison of Taisho 1510a and Taisho 1510b.

Chapter 1 Sanskrit Text, Chinese, Tibetan, English Translations.

Chapter 2 Analysis of the Vajracchedikā according to Vasubandhu (Taisho 1510 and compared with Kamalsīla's commentary).

Appendix II The Gilgit text of the Vajracchedikā by N.P. Chakravarti.

Section II Mahāyāna-vimśikā of Nāgārjuna.

Section III Navaślokī of Kambalapāda.

Section IV Catuḥstavasamāsārtha of Amṛtakara.

Section V Hetutattvopadeúa of Jetāri and Tarkasāpāna of Vidyākaraśānti with Introduction.

(1958) *Minor Buddhist Texts*, Part II.

First Bhāvanākarma of Kamalsīla.

Sanskrit and Tibetan text with introduction and English summary. This work represents a collection of Mahāyāna texts, found by G. Tucci in Tibet and in Nepal.

(1958) Preliminary Report on Archacological Survey in Swat (*East and West,* IX).

(1961) L' Afganistan dolla prehistoria (Al l'Islam Capalavari del Meseo de Kabul.).

(1971) *Minor Buddhist Text,* Part III.

Third Bhāvanākrama supplied from India, by Dr. Lokesh Chandra.

(1963) Oriental Notes I, II (*East and West,* Vol.13-14)

(1966) *Tibetan Folk Songs* (2nd.edn.Ascona)

(1967) *Tibet, Land of Snow* (Oxford, London, Calcutta, Bombay and New Delhi).

(1971) *Deb ther dmar po* with English translation.

(1978) *Trans-Himalayas*, New Delhi.

(1980) *The Religion of Tibet* (tr. from German and Italian by Geoffery Samuel, Routleage and Kegan Paul, London).

(D) On Nepal and the Himalayas

(1956) *Preliminary Report on Two Scientific Expeditions in Nepal*, Rome.

(1959) A Hindu Image in the Himalayan (*Asia Major* Vol. 7. New series, pp 170-75).

(1962) Nepal, the Discovery of Mallas (tr. from Italian.).

Lo-Che Rin-Chen-Bzan-Po as a Great Translator

15

Bimalendra Kumar

Giuseppe Tucci published his monograph on Rin-chen-bzan-po in Italian from Reale Accademia d'Italia, Rome in November 1932. This monograph was translated into English by Nancy Kipp Smith under the direction of Thomas J.Pritzker under *Indo-Tibetica* Vol.II, which has been edited by Prof. Lokesh Chandra and published from Aditya Prakashan, New Delhi in 1988. This Volume is a detailed study of Rin-chen-bzan-po and contains reproduction of the original biographical text in Tibetan. Details of the life and multi-dimensional work of Rin-chen-bzan po are available in his various biographies (*rnam-thar*) of which one composed by *Ye-shes-dpal* (Jñānaśrī), entiled '*Bla-ma-lotshsh-ba-chen-pohi rnam-pra-thar pah Dri ma-med-pa-shel-gyi 'phren zes bya-ba'* and translated by David L.Snellgrove and Tadeusz Skorupski as the *'Saving Cord of the Crystal Rosary'*, is significant one. In 1977, *Rdo-rje-tshe brtan* brought out '*Collected Biographical Material about Lo-Che Rin-chen-bzan-po and his subsequent Reembodiments'*. It reproduces manuscripts from the library of the Dkyil Monastery in Spiti. The *Blue Annals* of gZon-nu dpal by G.N. Roerich also contains valuable data on the great Lotsaba.

Rin-chen-bzan-po is being revered by Tibetans for his role in the 'Second Propagation' of Buddhism in Tibet. His personality is famous not only as the greatest founder of the temples and *Chos-khors* but also as profound scholar-translator in the overall contest of rise and development of Buddhism in Tibet. In this paper there is an humble attempt to discuss *Rin-chen-bzan* po as a great translator. The great translator is credited with having translated over 150 of the basic Buddhist texts from Sanskrit into Tibetan. Before discussing on this aspect, the life of Rin-chen-bzan po is mentioned here in a very brief manner.

According to Gos lotsaba gZon-nu-dpal, the great translator Rin-chen-bzan po was born in an Earth-male-Horse year and he was 85 years when Atisa came to Tibet. Thus, the Earth-Male-Horse year of his birth is to be taken as A.D. 950, which is just 329 year after the birth of Sron-btsan-sgam-po. At the age of thirteen, he was ordained by the Upadhyaya *Ye-s 'es-bzan-po*[1] and immediately afterwards he was sent to India at the order of King *Ye-s' es-hod*. He met Atisa in 1042 and he died in the wood-goat year i.e. in 1055 at the age of 98. While still a youth, he went to Kashmir and perfected himself in many systems of mysticism and in logic, under Pandit Gunamitra, Dharmashanta and Shraddhakaravarman.

Rin-chen-bzan po met the great Buddhist tantric schol and Siddha Naropa (956-1040 A.D.) at the latter's retreat house at Pullahari in the northern Kashmir and received instruction in meditation on *mahāmudrā*. From Pandit Kamalagupta he mastered many secrets of the tantric meditation. Thus, having stayed for seven years in Kashmir (976-983 A.D.), he attained profound scholarship in various fields of learning and tantric practice under various Pandits, Yogis and Siddhas. All the works that he studied in Kashmir, he rendered them in Bhoti on the birch back leaves (*bhojpatra*) and arranged them in the Pothis.

The most productive period of Rin-chen-bzan po's carrier covers a decade between 989-999 A.D. During that period, he not only founded temples and *Chos-khors*, but also headed the whole establishment of scholars and translators, who were engaged in the stupendous task of editing and translating Indian textual knowledge into Bhoti language not only at Tholing, but also at other *Chos-khors*. He was asked to go to Kashmir once again by the Royal Lama Ye-shes-od, so that he could bring home the books he had left with Shraddhakaravarman and also to bring with him some skilled artists. Again he came to Kashmir, and utilized his subsequent stay in guding the disciples and returned to his home country in 1005 A.D. with a contingent of thirty-two Kashmiri artists and many scholars, along with the books. He was designated as the chief priest (*dbuhi mchod-gnas*) and *Vajracharya (Rdorje Slobdpon)* of Tholing Chos-khor. The King honoured him with the coveted title of the Lotsaba, i.e., the great Translator - the highest title of scholarship for a Tibetan. The work of translating Buddhist texts into Bhoti was not only confined to Tholing, but each *Chos-khor* was agog with scholastic activities. In fact, the work of translating texts into Bhoti had become a national mission in the western Tibet of that age and even kings doned monastic robes and devoted themselves to the cause of Buddhist scholarship.[2]

Although the details of the work translated at different *Chos-khors* in that age is not known, but it should have been of stupendous magnitude, as may be inferred from the encyclopaedic collection preserved in *Kangyur* and *Tangyur*, in which works translated by the school of translators and Lotsabas under Rin-chen-bzan-po, were edited and compiled by Buton Rinpoche (*Ratnasiddhi*, 1290-1369 A.D.) in the 14th century (1340 A.D.).[3]

The Translation Procedures in Tibet

The Translations of the Buddhist texts went on very slowly during the seventh and the first half of the eighth century A.D. Large-scale translation of the texts were resumed at the time of Khri-srong lde-brtsan, and it continued till the reign of devout emperor Ral-pa-can (817-36) and his father. During the time of Ral-pa-can and his father Sad-na-legs, the translations were done in more. For the uniformity the older translations were revised. Under imperial auspices, a committee of Indian and Tibetan scholars was set up to establish uniformity in the translation of Buddhist technical terms.[4] In Tibet the average number of persons involved in translating a text seems to have been significantly smaller. For a given text, we commonly find one or two Tibetan translators collaborating with one or two Indian scholars.[5] There were some Indian scholars who mastered Tibetan sufficiently to be able to communicate in Tibetan. The well-known Indian scholar Smrtijnanakirti, active in central and eastern Tibetan early 11th Century A.D, translated many texts, mainly in the field of tantra. He even wrote a Tibetan grammar namely, *Smra-sgo*, combined with an auto-commentary.[6] On the other hand, a great many Tibetan scholars are known to have studied Indian languages and dialects to have travelled extensively in India, and to have studied under Indian masters. It seems that a number of Tibetan scholars, especially those active as translators, must have been able to communicate in some Indian languages.[7]

The scriptures introduced in the early days can be classified into two groups.[8] In the first, there are the texts translated specially by chosen and appointed persons (Lotsabas) working in collaboration with Chinese, Indians and Central Asians, and which were intended for the education of the monks after the foundation of the various religious communities. Second, there were general compendia, intended for the conversion of the public at large, such as the *dGe bcui mdo, rDo rje gcod pa, Sa lui ljang pa,* books which were, it seems, introduced by *Sang shi,*[9] and other short summaries of the teachings similar to those cited in the edicts of *Khri srong lde brtsan.*[10]

When Buddhism flourished again in Tibet in the latter part of the tenth century A.D., Buddhist translation activities were resumed with the cooperation of Tibetan and Indian scholars. New translations were produced with the help of contemporary Indian tradition. Rin-chen-bzan-po made the translation, which also included the revision of old translations, made during the reign of the great emperors. There were some recognised set of works for example, the *Vinaya* and its commentaries, but there was at that time no complete Canon, which needed but to be systematically translated in a scholarly way. Texts were collected and translated piece-meal in accordance with the individual's aptitude and propensities.[11] There was also necessary for Lotsaba to create a bit of his own language and style. It was not an easy matter, because a literary experience was still lacking or was just about to be established. There were many and diverse dialects, which were spoken there. Thus, a unified language comprehensible to all the provinces was necessary. Rin-chen-bzan po continued to revise and correct the works, started by Tibetan and Indians since the time of *Kri-sron-lde-btsan* and *Ral-pa-can*. He reproduced the ideas contained in the Buddhist texts in a matter that could be understood by all. He tried to bend marvellous construction of the Sanskrit sentence to a different syntax and find equivalents for the philosophical terms.

The Collaborators of Rin-chen-bzan-po

Rin-chen-bzan-po was associated with a number of collaborators, who can be divided into two categories-firstly his immediate masters (or teachers) in India who initiated him in the diverse Buddhist disciplines and experiences and secondly those who, through royal invitation, translated themselves in the Tibetan herimitages or in one of the many temples that the Lo-tsa-ba constructed, or rather had persuaded the munificent kings to construct.[12]

The *Deb-ther-snon-po* cites several references regarding many disciples of Rin-che-bzan-po, whether they were learned men or ascetics. The king Ye-s'es-hod had the Pandit Dharmapala of eastern India, from whom are derived three commentators of the *Vinaya*, that is Sadhupala, Gunupala, and Prajnapala, usually known as "the three palas" the school that esteemed from them was called the school of monastic rules of *stod*; Subhutis'risanti who translated the *Aṣṭasāhasrikā-prajñāpāramita*, his large commentary (*hgrel-chen*), and the *Abhisamayalankara* (*Mnon-patogs-pahi-rgyan*) with his commentary. The disciples of *Rin-chen-bzan-po*, on the other hand, continued the work of the master in three branches: *sūtra, Prajñāpāramitā* and *mantra*, all of them, the Lotsaba of *Rma*, *Dge-ba-blo gros* deserves to be mentioned. He translated the *Pramāṇavārttika (Tshad-ma-rnan-hgrel*), the commentary to this work written by the same author, that is by Dharmakirti (*Pramāṇavārttika-vritti*), the commentary of *Lha-dban-blo (Devendra Buddhi*) and the commentary of *Sakyabuddhi* (*Sakyablo*).[13]

Pupils gathered around the Lotsaba from every part of Tibet, not only from *Mnah-ris*, but also from *Dhus* and *Gtsan*. Among them *Gz' on-nu-dpal* records the lesser Lotsaba *Legs pahi-s,es-rab; Brtson-hgrus-rgyal-mtshan* of *Gur-s' in Man-nan; Gz' on-nu-ses-rab* of *Gra* and *Jnana* of *Skyi-nor*;[14] who were considered by *Rin-chen-bzan-po* as his favorite disciples. Four others were pupils of both the greater and the lesser Lotsaba *An-ston Grags-rin Spu-hrans, Rgya-ye-tshul, Dge-ses* of Gun, and *Dkon-mchog-brtsegs of Mar-yul*. In addition *Rgyan-pa Chos-blos* of *Rgyan-ro-speudmar in Myan-stod* was considered to be as the disciple of the lesser Lotsaba. He learned from Rin-chen-bzan-po the mystical system of the *Vajrodaya*.

Another disciple of the greater Lotsaba was *Sum-ston ye-hbar* of *S'ans* who for seven years studied with him.

According to *pad-ma-dkar-po, Legs-pahi-S 'es-rab*, Gz'on-nu-s' es-rab, ye-s' es-dban-phyug of *Skyi-nor* and *Britson-grus-rgyal-mtshan* of *Gur-s in* were the principal disciples of *Rin-chen-bzan-po*. The biography of Rin-chen-bzan-po records the name of his teacher namely now *Da-ka-ra-bar-ma* (21) now *Sra-ta ra-barma* (22), now *Tratakara* (25, 28), *now Tra-ta-kar-bar-ma* (26). The names are often so altered that it is difficult to recognize them. But, it is not difficult to recognize among such names that of the Pandita Sraddhakaravarman who had been invited by *Nor-bu-gling-po* there to explain the system of *Vajrodaya (rdo-rje-hbyun)*.

Some idea of the scholastic enterprise of the Great Lotsaba may be had from the lengthy bibliography of his works,[15] which he himself or in collaboration with other Tostabas and Indian translators rendered into Bhoti. These include eighteen treatises on the *Sutra* and *Tantra*, which form part of *Kangyur*, thirty-three works of commentary on *Tantras*, totalling of an enormous figure of 161 works. Among these, fourteen works are exclusively translated by him and, for remaining 147 works, he collaborated with other Lotsabas and Indian translators, among which mention may be made of :

1. Atisa (Dipankara Srijnana)
2. Shraddhakaravarman,
3. Padmakaravarman,
4. Subhashita,
5. Kamalagupta,
6. Dharmashribhadra.
7. Lotsaba Tshul-khrims-yon-tan,
8. Lotsaba Shes-rab-legs-pa,
9. Lotsaba Shakya-blo-gros (*Shakyamuni*)
10. Prajnakaravarman.
11. Gangadhara,
12. Buddhabhadra,
13. Janardhana,
14. Buddhasrishanti,
15. Prajnasrigupta,
16. Viryabhadra,
17. Tathagatarakshita,
18. Vijayashridhara,
19. Devakara,
20. Subhuti and
21. Kanakavarman.

The name of collaborator and translator has been given in each work. Although some of the works were translated exclusively by *Rin-chen-bzan-po*. The precise period of the collaborators and translators can be drawn. All these Pandits and Lotsabas, then are contemporaries of Rin-chen-bzan-po and their activity should therefore, be confined within a very precise time limit-the second half of the tenth century A.D. and until about the third quarter of the 11th century A.D.

The biography of *Rin-chen-bzan-po* does not agree with the informations, taken from the other sources. As for example, there is the mention among the masters of Rin-chen-bzan-po, *Jinamitra* and *S'ilendrabodhi*, who, as is well known, belong to the first period of Tibetan translations, since both lived at the time of Khri-sron-lde-btsan, collaborating together with Kluhi-rgyal-mtshan, Danas'ila etc.

Thus, it seems from the above discussions that how *Lo-che Rin-chen-bzan po* contributed fruitful for the spread of Buddhism and for producing a number of Indian texts into Tibetan, thus providing a religious exchange between Tibet and India. He create not only a literature but a new culture, or rather he gave Tibet a culture that it had never possessed before.

References

1. George N.Roeich, *The Blue Annals*, I & II, Motilal Banarasidas, Delhi, 1976, p.68.

2. O.C. Handa, *Tabo Monastery and Buddhism in the Trans-Himalaya,* Indus Publishing Company, New Delhi 1994. p. 72.

3. O.C. Handa, *Buddhist Monasteries in Himachal pradesh*, Delhi (1987), p.120.

4. Hoffman, Helmut, *Tibet: A Hand Book*, Indian University, Bloomington, p.202.

5. Verhagen, P.C., *A History of Sanskrit Grammatical Literature in Tibet,* Vol.I, ed. by Brill, Lieden, 1994, p.47.

6. *The Tibetan Tripitaka*, ed. by T.D. Suzuki, Tokyo 1955-61, title numbers 5784 and 5785.
7. Verhagen, P.C., *op. citt.*, p.48.
8. Tucci, G., *The Religions of Tibet*, London, 1970, p.7-8.
9. The common tradition is that *Sang Shi* was sent to China and to India, and that he took along with him from China some books and according to some, also a Hva san. Some say that he was a Tibetan and others a Chinese — G.Tucci, *Minor Buddhist Texts* II, Rome, 1958, pp.11-12.
10. Tucci, G., *The Tombs of the Tibetan Kings*, Rome, 1950, p.49.
11. Cf. D.L. Snellgrove, *Buddhist Himalaya*, Bruno Cassirer, Oxford, London, 1957, pp. 180-81.
12. Tucci, G., *Rin-Chen-bzan-po*, Aditya Prakshan, New Delhi, 1988, p. 26.
13. *Ibid.*, p. 29.
14. Jnana of *Khri-than* is considered as to have written *rnam-thar* of Rin-chen-bzan-po.
15. For the detailed list of works of Rin-chen-bzan-po, kindly see the Annexure-I

Annexure-I

List of the works translated by Rin-chen-bzan-po:

In Kangyur (*Sūtras* and *Tantras*)

1*. *Laghusamvaratantra*; Rin-chen-bzan-po.

2. Abhidhānottaratantra; Rin-chen-bzan-po., Dipankara srijnana.

3. *Sarvatathāgatakāyavākcittarahasyaguhyasamāja*; Rin-chen-bzan-po, Sraddhakaravarman.

4*. *Māyājālamahātantrarāja*; Rin-chen-bzan-po.

5*. *Śricandraguhyatilakamahātantrarāja*; Rin-chen-bzan-po.

6. *Sarvatathāgatatatvasangraha*; Rin-chen-bzan-po, Sraddhakaravarman.

7. Sarvarahasyatantrarāja; Rin-chen-bzan-po, Pmakaravarman.
8. *Śriparamādimahāyānakalparāja*; Rin-chen-bzan-po, *Sraddhakaravarman.*
9. *Āryavajrapāṇinīlāmbaradhāraṇilokavijaya*; Rin-chen-bzan- po, Dipankara Srijnana.
10. *Astasahasrikaprajnaparamita*; Rin-chen-bzan-po, Subhashita.
11. *Aṣhṭasāhasrikāprajñāpāramitā*; revised, Rin-chen-bzan-po, Dipankra Srijnana.
12. *Mahaparinrvāṇasūtra*; Rin-chen-bzan-po, Kamalagupta.
13. *Nairatmyaparipṛcchā*; Rin-chen-bzan-po, Kamalagupta.
14. *Ghaṇṭisūtra*; Rin-chen-bzan-po, Tshul-khrims-yon-tan, Dharmasribhadra.
15. *Abhiniskramanasūtra*; Rin-chen-bzan-po.Tshul-khrims-you-tan, Dharmasribhadra.
16. *Sumāgadhāvadāna*; Rin-chen-bzan-po, Tshul-khrims-yon-tan, Dharmasribhadra.
17. *Candraprabhāvadāna*; Rin-chen-bzan-po, Ses-rab-legs-pa, Dharmasribhadra.
18. *Srisenāvadāna*; Rin-chen-bzan-po, Ses-rab-legs-pa, Dharmasribhadra.

Commentaries on the Sutras (mdo- hgrel)

19. *Abhisamayālaṅkārāloka* of Haribhadra (trans.,revision); Rin-chen-bzan-po, Subhasita.
20. *Abhisamayālaṅkārāloka* of Haribhadra; Rin-chen-bzan-po, Dipankara.
21. *Durbodhāloka* (comm. on *Abhisamayālaṅkārāloka*); Rin-chen-bzan-po, Dipankara.
22. *Prajñāparamitānavaślokapiṇḍārtha*; Rin-chen-bzan-po, Sraddhakaravarman.
23. *Prajñāpāramitānavaślokapiṇḍārtha* (comm.); Rin-chen-bzan-po, Kamala-gupta.

24. *Hastabalaprakaraṇa*; Rin-chen-bzan-po, *Sraddhakaravarman.*

25. *Bodhicaryāvatāra*; Rin-chen-bzan-po, Dharmasribhadra, Sakya-blo-gros.

26. *Saṃvṛttibodhicittabhāvanopadeśavarṇasangraha*; Rin-chen-bzan-po, Padmakaravarman.

27. *Paramārthabodhicittabhāvanākramavarnasangraha*; Rin-chen-bzan-po *Padmakaravarman.*

28. *Pāramitāyānabhāvanākramopadeśa*;Rin-chen-bzan-po, Padmakaravarman.

29. *Dhyānasaddharmavyavasthāna*; Rin-chen-bzan-po, Dharmasribhadra.

30. *Dhyānasaddharmavyavasthāna*; (comm.); Rin-chen-bzan-po, Dharmasribhadra.

31. *Bodhisattvacaryāsaṅgrahapradīparatnamālā*; Rin-chen-bzan-po, Prajnakaravarman.

32. *Vimalapraśnottararatnamālā*;Rin-chen-bzan-po, Kamalagupta.

33. *Saptaguṇaparivarnanakathā*; Rin-chen-bzan-po, Gangadhara.

34. *Saṁbhāraparikathā*; Rin-chen-bzan-po, Gangadhara.

35. *Caturviparyayaparihārakathā*; Rin-chen-bzan-po, Buddhabhadra.

36. *Pañcavidhakāmaguṇopalammbhanirdeśa*; Rin-chen-bzan-po, Dharmasribhadra.

37. *Dhyānasaddharmavyavasthāna*; Rin-chen-bzan-po, Dharmasribhaḍra.

38. Yogāvatāra; Rin-chen-bzan-po, Dharmasribhadra.

39. *Yogāvataropadeśa*; Rin-chen-bzan-po, Janardana.

40. *Saptaguṇavarnanakathā*; Rin-chen-bzan-po, Kamalagupta.

41. *Triśaraṇagamanasaptati*; Rin-chen-bzan-po, Atisa.

42. *Prātimokṣabhāṣyasampramuṣitasmatraṇamatralekha*; Rin-chen-bzan-po, Janardana.

43. *Suvarṇavarṇāvadāna*; Rin-chen-bzan-po, Dharmasribhadra.
44. *Saptaguṇavarnanakathā*; Rin-chen-bzan-po, Gangadhara.
45. *Supthadeśanāparikathā*; Rin-chen-bzan-po, Atisa.
46. *Dṛṣṭāntamālya*; Rin-chen-bzan-po, Dharmasribhadra.
47. *Aṣṭāṅgahṛdayasamhitā*; Rin-chen-bzan-po, Janardana.
48. *Padārthachandrikā*; (comm.of *Astangahrdayasamhita*); Rin-chen-bzan-po, Janardana.
49. *Dhūpayogaratnamālā;* Rin-chen-bzan-po, Janardana.
50. *Aṣṭapadikṛitadhupayoga*; Rin-chen-bzan-po, Janardana.
51. *Śālihotriyaśvayurvedasamhitā*; Rin-chen-bzan-po, Dharmasribhadra, Buddhasrisanti.

Commentaries on the Tantras (Rgud-hgrel)

52. *Viśeṣastavaṭikā*; Rin-chen-bzan-po, Janardana.
53. *Devātiśayastotraṭikā*; Rin-chen-bzan-po, Janardana.
54. *Kāyatrayastotravivaraṇa*; Rin-chen-bzan-po, Sraddhakaravarman.
55. *Varṇanārhavarṇane Bhagavato Budddhasya stotre asakyastava*; (13th chapter); Rin-chen-bzan-po, Padmakaravarman.
56. *Ekottarikāstotra*; Rin-chen-bzan-po,Dharmasribhadra.
57. *Sugatapañcatrimsatstotra*; Rin-chen-bzan-po, Padmakaravarman.
58. *Desanāstava*; Rin-chen-bzan-po, Buddhakaravarman.
59*. *Buddhābhiṣeka-nāma-stotra*; Rin-chen-bzan-po.
60. *Pañcatathāgatastava*: Rin-chen-bzan-po, Sraddhakara (varman).
61. *Saptatathāgatastotra*; Rin-chen-bzan-po, Sraddhakara (varman).
62. *Suramanojña* (with commentary on *Sricakrasamvara*); Rin-chen-bzan-po, Dharmasribhadra.
63. *Sribhagavadabhisamaya*; Rin-chen-bzan-po, raddhaka-ravarman.

64. *Bhagavacchricakrasamvaramaṇḍalavidhi*; Rin-chen-bzan-po, Buddhasrisanti.

65. *Bhagavacchricakrasamvaramaṇḍalavidhi* Rin-chen-bzan-po, Dharmashribhadra.

66. *Herukāviśuddhi*; Rin-chen-bzan-po, Sraddhakaravarman.

67. *Herukasādhana*; Rin-chen-bzan-po, Dharmasribhadra.

68. *Shricakrasamvarasādhanā*; Rin-chen-bzan-po,Atisha.

69. *Bhagavadabhisamaya*; Rin-chen-bzan-po, Atisa.

70. *Cakrasamvaravistaraprabandha*; Rin-chen-bzan-po, Atisa.

71. *Vajrayoginistotra*; Rin-chen-bzan-po, Atisa

72. *Catuḥpithāyogasādhanatantrasādhanopāyikā*; Rin-chen-bzan-po, Kamalagupta.

73. *Tattvopadeśa*; Rin-chen-bzan-po, Kamalagupta.

74. *Sarvabuddhasamāyogatantrapañjikā*; Rin-chen-bzan-po, Sraddhakaravarman.

75. *Sarvabuddhasamayoga*; Rin-chen-bzan-po, Sraddhakaravarman, Dharmasribhadra.

76. *Mṛtyuvancanopadeśa*; Rin-chen-bzan-po, Atisa.

77 *Pradipoddyotana* (comm.on *Guhyasamāja*); Rin-chen-bzan-po, Sraddhakaravarman.

78. *Saḍaṅgayogaṭīkā*; Rin-chen-bzan-po, Sraddhakaravarman.

79. *Vajrajapaṭikā*; Rin-chen-bzan-po, Sraddhakaravarman.

80. *Jñānavajrasamuccayatantrodbhavasaptālaṅkāravimocana*; Rin-chen-bzan-po, Sraddhakaravarman.

81. *Piṇḍikṛtasādhanā*; Rin-chen-bzan-po, Sraddhakaravarman.

82. *Sūtramelapaka* (commentary on Guhyasamaja); Rin-chen-bzan-po. Dharmasribhadra.

83. *Guhyasamājamaṇḍalavidhi*; Rin-chen-bzan-po, Subhasita.

84. *Pancakrama*; Rin-chen-bzan-po, Sraddhakaravarman. Kamalagupta.

85. *Svādhiṣṭhānakramaprabheda*; Rin-chen-bzan-po, Sraddhakaravarman. Kamalagupta.

86. Abhisambodhikramopadeśa; Rin-chen-bzan-po, Sraddhakaravarman, Kamalagupta.

87. *Amṛtakuṇḍalisādhanā*; Rin-chen-bzan-po, Sraddhakaravarman, Kamalagupta.

88. *Mahāvajradharapathakramopadeśa*-amṛtaguhya; Rin-chen-bzan-po, Dharmasribhadra.

89. *Homavidhi*: Rin-chen-bzan-po, Sraddhakaravarman, Dharmasribhadra.

90. *Guhyasamājamaṇḍaladevakayastotra*; Rin-chen-bzan-po, Sraddhakaravarman.

91. *Srāddhapralapastava*; Rin-chen-bzan-po, Prajnasrigupta.

92. *Guyasamājavivaraṇa*; Rin-chen-bzan-po, Sraddhakaravarman.

93*. *Mukhāgama*; Rin-chen-bzan-po.

94. *Samantabhadrasādhanā*; Rin-chen-bzan-po, Sraddhakaravarman.

95. *Guhyasamājamaṇḍalavidhi*; Rin-chen-bzan-po, Padmakaravarman.

96. *Samantabhadravṛtti*; Rin-chen-bzan-po, Varyabhadra.

97. *Samantabhadrasādhanavṛti*; Rin-chen-bzan-po, Sraddhakaravarman.

98. *Muktitilakavyākhyāna*; Rin-chen-bzan-po, kamalagupta.

99. *Guhyasamājamaṇḍalavidhi-ṭīkā*; Rin-chen-bzan-po, Viryabhadra.

100. *Guhyasamājabhisamayasādhanā and Maṇḍalavidhi*; Rin-chen-bzan-po, Sraddhakaravarman.

101* *Priyasādhanā*; Rin-chen-bzan-po.

102. *Akshobhayavajrasādhanā*; Rin-chen-bzan-po, padmakara-varman.

103. *Suvisistasādhanopāyikā*; Rin-chen-bzan-po, Viryabhadra.

104. *Guhyasamājalokesvarasādhanā*; Rin-chen-bzan-po, Atisa.

105. *Abhisekaprakaraṇa*; Rin-chen-bzan-po, Tathagataraksita.

106. *Guhyasamājapañjikā*; Rin-chen-bzan-po, Vijayasridhara, Sraddhakaravarman.

107. *Yamārisādhana*; Rin-chen-bzan-po, Atisa.

108. *Vajrabhairavatantrapañjikā*; Rin-chen-bzan-po, Tathagataraksita.

109. *Deviprabhādharādhiṣṭhāna*; Rin-chen-bzan-po, Devakara

110*. *Jñānasiddhisādhanopāyikā*; Rin-chen-bzan-po.

111. *Vajrayānasthulapatti*; Rin-chen-bzan-po, Padmakaravarman.

112. *Kosalalaṅkāra*; Rin-chen-bzan-po, Dharmasribhadra.

113. *Vajradhātumandalasarvadevavyavasthāna*; Rin-chen-bzan-po, Padmakaravarman.

114. *Sankṣiptamaṇḍalasutravṛtti*;Rin-chen-bzan-po, Sraddhakaravarman.

115*. *Tattvasaṅgraha-ṭīkā*; Rin-chen-bzan-po.

116. *Paramādivṛtti*; Rin-chen-bzan-po, Padmakaravarman.

117. *Paramādiṭīkā*: Rin-chen-bzan-po, Sraddhakaravarman.

118*. *Māyājāla-ṭīkā*; Rin-chen-bzan-po.

119. *Māyājāla-pañjikā*; Rin-chen-bzan-po, Sraddhakaravarman.

120. *Sarvavajrodaya*; Rin-chen-bzan-po, Buddhasrisanti.

121*. *Trailokyavijayamaṇḍalopāyikā*; Rin-chen-bzan-po.

122 *Pratisthāvidhi*: Rin-chen-bzan-po,Sraddhakaravarman.

123 *Karuṇodaya*; Rin-chen-bzan-po, Sraddhakaravarman.

124 *Pratisthāvidhi*; Rin-chen-bzan-po, Dharmasribhadra.

125 *Homavidhi*; Rin-chen-bzan-po, Sraddhakaravarman.

126 *Nāmasangitivṛtti*; Rin-chen-bzan-po, Sraddhakaravarman.

127 *Mañjuśrīnāmasaṅgitiṭīkā*; Rin-chen-bzan-po, Sraddhakaravarman.

128. *Sarvadurgatiparisodhanamaṇḍalasādhanopāyikā*; Rin-chen-bzan-po, Subhutisribhadra.

129. *Sarvadurgatiparisodhanapretahomavidhi*; Rin-chen-bzan-po, Kankavarman.

130. *Sarvasuddhisamskārasūtrapaṇḍitavidhi*; Rin-chen-bzan-po, Sraddhakaravarman.

131. *Mahāvairocanābhisambodhisambaddhatantrapūjāvidhi*. Rin-chen -bzan-po, Padmakaravarman.

132. *Vajravidāraṇidharaṇīṭīkā*; Rin-chen-bzan-po, Sraddhakaravarman.

133. *Vajravidāraṇidharanivyākhyānabṛhaṭṭikā*; Rin-chen-bzan-po, Sraddhakaravarman.

134. *Vṛttipradīpa*; Rin-chen-bzan-po, Sraddhakaravarman.

135*. *Vṛttipradīpa*; (revision); Rin-chen-bzan-po.

136. *Āryamañjughosastotra*; Rin-chen-bzan-po, Sraddhakaravarman.

137. *Sahasrabhujāvalokiteśvarasādhanā*; Rin-chen-bzan-po, Atisa.

138. *Sthiracakrabhāvanā*; Rin-chen-bzan-po, Viryabhadra.

139. *Arpachanasādhanā*; Rin-chen-bzan-po, Kamalagupta.

140. *Nāgesvararājasādhanā*; Rin-chen-bzan-po, Atisa.

141. *Nayatrayapradīpa*; Rin-chen-bzan-po, Padmakaravarman.

142. *Tattvasiddhiprakaraṇa*, Rin-chen-bzan-po, Atisa.

143. *Tattvāvatāra*; Rin-chen-bzan-po, Padmakaravarman.

144. *Mantranayāloka*; Rin-chen-bzan-po, Padmakaravarman.

145. *Tattavasārasaṅgraha*; Rin-chen-bzan-po,, Janardana.

146. *Yogānuttaratantrārthavatārasaṅgraha*; Rin-chen-bzan-po, Sraddharavarman.

147. *Guhyapañcāsikā*; Rin-chen-bzan-po, Padmakaraovarman.

148. *Madhyamabhagatrayavidhi*; Rin-chen-bzan-po, Sraddhakaravarman.

149*. *Jalabalividhi*; Rin-chen-bzan-po.

150*. *Māhamudrāyogavatarapindartha*; Rin-chen-bzan-po.

151. *Nāgabalividhi*; Rin-chen-bzan-po, Atisa.

152. Bālipujavidhi; Rin-chen-bzan-po, Atisa.

153. *Dandakabhagavachakrasamyarastotra*; Rin-chen-bzan-po, Viryabhadra.
154. *Vajrayoginisadhana*; Rin-chen-bzan-po, Atisa.
155. *Pindikramasadhana*; Rin-chen-bzan-po, Sraddhakaravarman.
156. *Nilāmbaravajrapanisādhana*; Rin-chen-bzan-po, Atisa.
157. *Vajradharavajrapanikarmasadhana*; Rin-chen-bzan-po, Atisa.

158*. *Vajravidaranimandalavidhi*; Rin-chen-bzan-po.

159 *Karmākarastotra*; Rin-chen-bzan-po, Sraddhakaravarman.

160. *Yamarisadhana*; Rin-chen-bzan-po, Atisa.
161. *Bhumisutra*; Rin-chen-bzan-po, Padmakaravarman.

1. The list is based on the list reproduced by Tucci, *Indo-Tibeica*, Delhi (1988), Vol. II, pp.40-49 and O.C. Handa, *Tabo Monastery and Buddhism in the Trans-Himalaya*, Delhi (1994), pp. 134-41.

* Translation exclusively done by Rin-chen-bzan-po.

Food and Drink in Pali Canon 16

Madhusudan Mallik

Food is an element of life which frees man from the pain of hunger and sustains and maintains his life. It lifts him from barbarism to humanism and forms the basis of civilization. It leads him from activity to creativity and on to divinity. It differentiates individuals from individuals race to race and from country to country. It is various in different seasons. Man starts his food from nuts, fruits and roots and then comes to the tests of flesh. He ends his food in the use of fires in the cooking of meat to make himself healthy, wealthy and wise.

Food in Buddhism

Buddha did not place any restriction on food. A man can eat fish or flesh but he will not eat them if it is prepared simply to serve him. Some rules were framed about food — not to take food at improper times (*Vikālabhojana*).

Varieties of Food

The Jatakas refer to a variety of food. It recommends 18 kinds of flavoured food that could be prepared (J.i.186, 26)

1. Cereals

   Rice, Wheat, Barley

2. Pulses
   Mugga, masa, kalaya, kulattha etc.
3. Dairy Products
   Milk, butter, cearified-butter, butter-milk, yaghuart.
4. Vegetables *Sake* etc.
5. Meat
6. Fruits
   Mango, plantain, coconut, date, grapse etc.
7. Milk product
8. Sweets
9. Spice

Rules of Diet

Buddha emphasized the importance of the purity of food. He advised his followers to take food after cleaning the teeth with a tooth-pick (Vin.i.46). Food touched by a man of low breed does not defile it. Moderation in eating (*bhojane mattunnata*) is a golden mean. Storing of food in ordinary time is prohibited (M.vi.5.). Rich food is as far as possible to be avoided. Eating together with three persons (*tika bhojana*) and taking meal with the masses (*ganabhojana*) are to be eschewed. Rice-milk (*yagu*) in the morning, rice and curry at mid-day and slight repast with ghee, butter, oil and honey or molasses in the afternoon, were the rules. No food should be taken at the improper time *vikala bhojana* (ch. Xii).

Art of Cooking

The art of cooking was regarded as so prominent as to be regarded as one of the twenty-four different kinds of occupations in the country. It's importance was emphasized by Buddha to Ajatasattu. The Buddha had a separate dining-room (*Upatthanasala*-Vin.1.49, D.ii.119) at Vesali and also store-house (*Kappabhumi*). Food was also available in the market (*daniyaghara*-J.iii.287). In the Vinaya we can trace the existence of the post of a distributor of food (*Khajjabhajaka*, Vin.ii.136). Rice-kitchen (daniy-ghara) also existed. All these testify to the existence of culinary art.

Classification of Food

Food was classified into four groups :

(1) Soft food (Bhojaniya)

(2) Boiled rice (odana), boiled mixture of barley and beans (kammasa) parched barley meal (satthu), meat, macctna Fish.

(3) Hard food (khadaniya)

(4) Roots, stocks, leaves, flowers, fruits etc.

Food is also divided into four kinds:
asita, pita, khayita and sayita

Food is of two types

- Kabalimkahara (m.1.48)
- Kanabhakkha (m.I.78) eating husk-powder, a practice of certain ascetics.

Utencils

They were of various types. They are sometimes taken as eighteen different kinds made up of iron, copper, bronze, lead, silver, gold, precious metals, ivory, horn, cloth, leather, stone, conch-shells, wood, clay, brass, skin etc.

The Buddhist monks usually used utencils, made of copper, wood and clay, utencils of gold, silver and precious metals were used by the rich. The common people used copper, wood or skin vessels. The poor only allowed to use of water vessels made of brass, wood or skin (Cull.V.16.2). The ordinary uses of utencils are bhingara (J.i.85) a water jar, *pitakam* a basket (Vin.22.54) *kumbhi* (Th.Ii.283) a large round pot, pariyoga, a cauldron (Miln.118) cf. kadapiya a pan (J.V.252); *gopitaka* Vassel for hard food.

Stands made of wood, stone or brick to keep water. There were eight different kinds of strainers:

Parissavana, a water strainer, a filter (Vin.i.209) *dhammaraka* (Vin.ii.48) proper or regular water pot i.e. with a filter for strining water used by the ascetics.

Cereals

Rice is the staple food throughout the length and breadth of India. The Buddhists mentioned several varieties of rice (M.i.59) *vihi* (Skt. Vrihi (J.i.429) *Sali* (D.i.105) *amaka-dhanna*, *lohitaka* (Miln. 352) red rice etc. Superior quality of rice was enjoyed by the rich while the poor had to remain satisfied with the poor quality (J.i.486), three years old rice was liked by the people but the price stood in the way of their enjoyment.

Different Types of Rice

Laja (J.iii.580) fried rice , *Odana* (Vin.ii.214) boiled rice, *Payasa* (3.1.50) milk rice. Rice was provided at public rest houses (D.I.105). A mixture of rice and seasamin was very popular (J.iii.425) *Tilodana*, and sukara sali (J.vi.532) a kind of wild rice also existed - we have rice field (A.1.241) *sukarasali* (J.vi.532) a kind of wild rice also existed. We have rice field (A.i.241) Salikkhetta with ripening young rice. Sali with varieties gabbha (Dh.A.i.87) *Sali ratta* (Th.I.208) Kanajaka (J.v.230) and Mahasali boiled rice is usually preferred hot *(bhattam sampadetva+supavyanjana sampannam unnhe bhattam vaddhetva)*. Cooked rice *jhamaka-bhatte* (J.iv.43) not usually eaten alone, but with soup (pulses) and vegetables. Rice dishes with meat or flesh was a favourite menu. Rice milk was favourable at the breakfast. Sometimes honey was mixed with rice. *Udamantha* or *Udakamantha* was a variety prepared out of fried rice (*bhujiya*). *Nivapatina* (J.I.250) 'grass' was food for the poor. *Kammasa-Kammasa-pinda* (J.No.415) Ved. *Kalmasa* 'a course food for the poor'. *Satthu* (vi.ii.116) cf-skt. saktu. There were baker's shop. Satthu-apana (V.vi.365). *Satthubhasto* (J. iii. 346).

Pulses (beans)

Kalaya skt., Kalaya (M.i.245) a kind of pea, chick pea. It is higher than a kidney bean (mugga) and smaller than the kernel of a jujubi (*Kulatthi*)

Kulattha — a kind of vetch (Miln. 267).

Masa (Miln. 267), Ved masa (*Phaseolus indica*) closely related to another species mugga (Vin. iii. 64) words connected with masa — Khatta a field of bean (VV. A. 308).

Mugga — Ved. Mudge, a kind of kidney bean, mugga. (Visu. 27)

Samaka (J.iii.44) a kind of millet, *Panicum Framen taceum*.

Vegetables

There were various types of vegetables. Saka (M.i.78) was the common type and there were grounds for cultivation of vegetables. There is also reference to various types saka vatthu (J.I.466) saka pannavanna (J.v.206), vegetables were sold at the gate of Uttra Pancala (J.i.139).

Buddha preferred a leafy vegetable to his followers to stocks of lotus (bisa), to roots of lotus, salika 'Long bottle-ground', alabu 'brinjal', The Buddhist nuns were fond of onions but due to bad odour they were prohibited.

Fruits

There were various kinds of fruits. Seven kinds of medicinal fruits are mentioned in the Vinaya (Vin. i.201), Vi2.

Vilanga (Vin.i.20) cf. Sft.-Vilanga, the plant *Erycibe paniculata*; *Pippala* for usual Pipphali skt. Pippli 'peepper' (Vin.i.201). There were various kinds of fruits (Phalaphala)— amba (J.i.416) panasa etc..

Marica 'black pepper'; Haritaka (D.ii.342) Pot-herb. Vibhitaka (Vin.i.201) the plant terminalia belerica, beleric myrobolam Dice was made form its fruits which are also used as medicine.

Amalaka (Vin.i.201) emblic myrobalan, phyelan thus emblica.

Fruits baskets (Phala-pacchi (J.vi.560) also Phala-puta (J.vi.236) are also mentioned. The office of a fruit distributor (Phalabhajaka (VI.iv.38) an official in the monastry. Water and made of a kind of gruel, it is used as an emetic (J.i.419), a medicinal plant (J.V.420).

Yagu

Ved yavagu, rice-gruel, (Vin.1.46). It has five good qualities. It is good for hunger, thirst and allays wind, cleans the blader, helps to digest any undigested food. It is often eaten bhojja (J.i.270).

Godhuma (Dh.A.i.163), wheat, usually mentioned with yava 'spelt'.

Yava

In the Buddhist texts, we have various words connected with Yava 'corn in general' and 'barley in particular'. Viz., Yava kalapi (S.iv.204) 'a sheaf of barley', Yava khetta (Vin.iv.47) corn field, Yava kammasa 'barley gruel', Yava suka (A.i.8) 'beard of corn' (barley). This Yava was the staple food of the Vedic Aryans one of the earlist of grains cultivated by man. Some scholars interpret it as corn.

Gula

Sugar, molasses (Vin.i.210) is prepared from sugar cake (gula pittham picharikam pi pakkhipanti). It was an important item of food which Buddha recommended for his followers (imani kho panca bhesajjani, seyyathidana sappi navanita bhesajjani (Vin.vi.199).

Spices

'Marica (Vin.i.20) 'Black peeper', Jiraka (J.i.244) 'Cummin seed', Halidda (M.i.127) 'tumeric', Sasapa (S.ii.137) a smustard seed.

Lavana (Miln. 112), salt, cf. also lona (Vin. i.202) ambila (Miln.5b) sour, acid, lavana, kasaya, madhura and one mugga (J.i.274) cf. Ved. Mudga, a kind of kidney-bean, *phaseol us* mungo, frequently combined with masa (Vin.iii.64). It is larger than a sasapa and smaller than a kalaya a kind of pea (J.ii.75).

Beverages

Buddha recommended eight kinds of beverages (anujanami bhikkhave atthapanani ambapanam etc. rose apple, plantain fruits. Ripe mango juice, grapes, edible root of water lily, honey, pharusaka fruits and cocoanut.

Oil

Castor seed (eranda) linseed (atasi) clarified butter, mustard, seasame, fat, kusumbha (J.v.211) the sunflower. tila, Ved, tila, sesame plant and its seed, out of which oil is prepared, *(Sesamum indicum)*. It is combined with very important articles of food (J.v.167). It was used by the poor people (J.i.340).

Sasapa (skt. Sarsapa), a mustard seed. (Sn. 625) Sasapa kutta 'mustard powder' (Vin.i.205).

Dairy Products

Khira, skt. *Ksira* milk (Vin.i.243) sometimes mentioned in combination with *dadhi*, *Navanita sappi* and *sappiman* data are the constituent materials for food (kabalinkahara-Vin.iv. 138). Terms are like milk-rice, buddhakhira (Sn.18) one who has boiled milk'. Khirodana 'milk rice' (boiled) are mention there is also reference of calf sucking milk (vaccho matari khiropako (J.vi.357). A cow is sometimes distinguished as milk-giver (khironika (S.i.174). We have also referances of Navanita, Ved *navanitan* 'fresh butter' cf. Beng. Nani (Pug. 69.70); Takka (Vin. i. 244) 'butter-milk'. It is made by churning dadhi (J.i.340); Ghata (Miln.41) 'clarified butter', skt. Ghatasana (J.i.470); Sappi (D.i.9) 'ghee, clarified butter' , skt. *arpin*. It had three qualities (Miln.332); and Go-rasa (Dh. A.1.158) 'produce of the cow'.

Sweet

Honey, molases, suger etc. formed the mainfold items of sweets.

Madhu (J.i.157) 'honey' was of three kinds—small bee, big bee and of a variety called kuttiya. There is also the mention of Madhu laja (J.V.214.281) 'sweet fried rice'.

Icchu

Ved, iksu, sugarcane (Vin.iv.35) was of considerable use. Juice of 'ikkhu' was also extracted (Vin.i.346) and Ucchu-khetta (J.i.339) 'sugarcane field' was required to be procted. Sugar-mills (ucchu-yantra, (J.i.339) justify the exitance of abundant sugar in the country. In the Vinaya we get the word gulakarana means 'a suger factory' (vin.i.276).

Drink

Plain water, milk, fruit-juice syrup made from grapes, dates, tamarinds, wine, liquor etc. Drinks of one kind or other was current in ancient Indian from times immemorial. Water was usually regarded as the best of drinks yet aloholic and fermented drinks had their own places. On festive and ceremonial occasions drinking to excesses was not uncommon.

Drinking Water

Cool water drawn from mountain spring are conductive to health (*atthi me paniyam sitalam abhatam girigahvara tato piva maharaja, sace tvam abhisambhasati*, jatakano.540)

There were also eight kinds of drinks — *anujanassi bhikkhave atthapanani, ambapanam coco panam mocapanam matthupanam mudditopanam pharusakapanam.*

Intoxicating Drinks

The Jatakas refer to the wide prevalence of intoxicating drinks like sura, meraya etc. viz., *suram pibanti, merayam pibanti* (A.ii.54). There were taverns (filled with crowds where wine was kept filled up within jars and sold freely (J.i.253, nos.43.481). The owners employed persons to help them in their business (J.i.251-52). It is remarkable that the owners of these taverns are not low class people but 'setthis' owing vast landed properties. It is not usual that wives also accompanied their husband to the taverns (J.iv.114). Illisa, a merchant whose wealth ran upto 80 cross went to taverns for drinks. On festive occasions drinking of wine was rampant. A festival called '*Sura-Nakkhatta*' permitted people to drink unrestricted wine and to fest and dance (J.i.342, 489). The Jataka (kusubha, No. 512) refers to a king who drank in its court surrounded by his courtiers before the citizen who also drank. It is reported that *Canda Pajjata* was in a drinking mood for three days when Udayana, king of Avanti was brought alive (Dh.A.i.1930.)

Buddha did not permit his followers to take to strong drink expect under illness (Vin.Vi.1.160). The evils of drinking were also recognised. Drink of strong liquire was also prohibited (A.ii.208). Monks were not allowed to drink *sura, mereya* etc.

Meat Dite

During the time of the Buddha meat of various kinds was prevalent. There was no bar on the eating of flesh except under extraneous circumstances. It is said that there existed a meat market at Mithila (J.408) and numerous slaughter-houses (J.V.408, J.V.62). Selling of fish was not unknown in various places (J.292). There was no restriction with regard to fish eating. It was freely eaten irrespective of the rich and the poor (J.V.242-43). Meat and fish are mentioned together in many places (J.iii.337). Meat-eating was very popular in Buddha's time. He did not interfere with this practice except for the Bikkhus who could accept it only as alms (M.V.23, 10-15). In the Mahaparinibana Sutta Buddha is found eating pig-meat at the house of Cunda, the smith (D.ii.127; Ud.Viii.37). Buddha also praised cooked meat at the house of a householder (J.ii.262).

The Buddhist literature is replete with various sorts of killings Cattle (M.i.364), Buffalo (J.ii.26), Chakala (J.vi.237), and Sukara (D.i.5). There were bands of professional hunters. Existence of slaughtering houses are not wanting (M.I.354). Meat was taken to the open markets by carts to be sold (J.315). Meat was also favourite dite with the king (J.i.242). Brahman as depicted in Pali Canon are found relishing various food including fish and meat (J.i.166, No.18). Buddha forbade the use of flesh of the following animals — elephant, horse, dog, lion, tiger, panther, bear and a hynea (M. v.vi. 23). A particular profession called flower existed to kill animals. Deer meat was carried to towns and cities by carts for sale in the open market (J.iii.49) pig-eating was also a familier dish with the people. It was generally killed on the wedding day for the marriage-feast (J.i.196, J.ii.419). The high and low in the country were found of it. Slaughter of cattle including cows continued but a tendency to revere the cow manifested itself in some quarter. Place of slaughtering cow (*goghatakasunam*) and implements to kill the cows are also found (M.i.364). The reference to be slaughter of cows or oxen during the time of the famine (J.ii.635) is found. Jatakas refer to the flesh of some birds — pegion (J.No.277), geese (J.214), herons (214) peacocks, crows and cocks (J.ii.412) as estables. It is strange how the ascetics ate and relished lizards and snakes — *mayam ajja godha potakam piva, labhimha iman nagarajam vadhitva khadissama*(J.v.163). Outside Varanasi vension was also sold (J.vi.62).

Inspite of the doctorine of non-violence, during this period non-vegetarian diet was popular and the practice of meat-eating was not affected. But Buddha had no objection except eating cows meat.

Practice of killings

Reference of *Goghataka* (D.ii.294) 'killings of cows', pigs, sheep, existence of slaughtering-houses *suna* (Vin.i.20) are also traced. '*Sunaghara Sunakaghara', Sukarika* 'a pig killer' are also found.

Conclusion

Rice played a role more important than barley or wheat. Various milk-products, fruits and vegetables of all sorts of general use, syrup of all were widely current. Drinking was rampant. On festive occasions it was unthinkable. Buddha imposed no restrictions provided it helped to sustain life.

List of Abbreviations

The edition of the texts referred to are those published by the Pali Text Society, London. The Roman and the Arabic figures in the references, refer respectively to the volume and the page numbers.

A	=	Auguttara Nikaya
D	=	Digha-Nikaya
Dh.	=	Dhammapada

Dh. A	=	Dhammapada Althakatha
It	=	Itivuttaka
J.	=	Jataka
M	=	Majjhima Nikaya
Miln.	=	Milinda Pañha
Mnvs.	=	Mahavastu
Pug.	=	Puggala Pannatti
S.	=	Sanyutta Nikaya
Sn.	=	Sutta Nipata
Th.	=	There Gatha
Th ii	=	Theri Gatha
Ud.	=	Udana
Vin	=	Vinaya Pitaka
Vism	=	Visuddhimagga
Vv. A.	=	Vimanavatthu Atthakatha.

Stupa in Early Buddhist Religion and Art

17

Ananda Chandra Sahoo

Gautama Buddha also known as Tathagata; i.e. he who has arrived at the truth, was the founder of Buddhism. The Buddhist traditions, on the other hand, suggest the existence of twentyfive Buddha, in which Gautama Buddha was the twentyfifth and the last[1]. Apart from the traditional accounts there are certain archaeological evidences which suggest about the twentyfourth Buddha; i.e., *Kanakamana Buddha*. *Kanakamana Buddha*, to whom we shall turn later, was the only other Buddha in memory of whom stupa has also been dedicated. In the present study the focus will be on the origin and spread of Buddhism with reference to its early architectural phenomenon — the stupa. During the life time of the Buddha, the followers found in him their supreme hero. However, after his great demise, the samgha was almost immediately confronted with many challenges. The followers met together and tried their best to keep the samgha away from being disintegrated. In the process, the concept of worship found favour, to which Gautama Buddha never vouched for. As it has been observed Buddha was only a preacher, a guide to truth; neither divine nor supernatural[2].

Gradually the traditional method of representing a cult object through a visual phenomenon was adopted by the Buddhists. In early Buddhism, the anthropomorphic representation of the Lord was not a sudden development. In this regard the evidences are in abundance in the early Buddhist art. The process evolved alongwith the traditional evolutionary method; i.e., from amorphic representation to aniconic, from aniconic representation to zoomorphic, from zoomorphic representation to therio-anthropomorphic, and from therioanthropomorphic representation to anthropomorphic forms. The first of the above forms is invisible and incomprehensible, whereas the rest are of visual forms. The present study evolves around the second form, viz., the aniconic form.

It is true that Gautama Buddha never advocated in favour of cult worship in his eighty years of existence in this world. However, in advocating for a moral and ethical reform of the entire world, he asked his followers to take the '*pabhajjā*' and the '*upasampadā*' ordinations; i.e., to get out of the society and to arrive at the life of the '*saṁghā*' or the order of the monks and nuns[3]. Thus the monastic life and organization received the attention of the master in his life time, and in this system, probably was the origin of the tradition of the worship. After the demise of the Buddha gradually his aniconic forms became the object of worship within his followers. In the beginning the aniconic forms such as, *Caitya* tree (*Bodhi-druma*), Umbrella (*Chhatra*), feet (*Pāduka*), wheel (*Dharma-cakra*) are most usual[4]. These apart, other icon611onic forms such as, stupa, alter or throne (*Bodhi-manda*, *vajrāsana*), Cushion, a piece of stone, foot stool, foot impression were most important and frequent representation. In early Buddhist art and architecture of Bharhut, Sanchi, Bodhagaya and Ajanta the above mentioned symbols have been repeatedly carved. These symbols represent the presence of the Buddha to which the followers pay their obeisance. In the following pages we shall concentrate our discussion on the most widely popular object of the aniconic tradition, i.e., the *stūpa*.

Generally in its structural form the *stūpa* is a hemispherical solid structure (*aṇḍa*) of brick with a truncated top resting on a low circular base (*medhi*). The truncated top (*harmikā*) is provided with a railing (*vedikā*). From the center of the harmika rises the shaft (*yaṣṭhi*), which supports the Umbrella (*chatra*), which in its the center of the hemispherical structure and on the top of the circular base, is kept the relic within a casket, which is the most sacred object, obviously not visible. At a distance on the ground level and as well as on the top outer edge of the base the *stūpa* is provided with railings. The space in between the railing and the outer edge of the circular base or the hemispherical dome is used as the passage for circumambulation (*pradakshiṇapatha*). At four cardinal points the stupa is provided with four entry-gates. These entry-gates, in important example are provided with elaborately carved gateways (*toraṇa*).

The *stūpa* as a free standing monument became the nerve centre in early Buddhist religion and art. In general, the tradition of the *stūpa* is infact pre-Buddhist [5]. As the ashes of important deceased were burid under a tope which is '*thupa*' in pali and *stūpa* in Buddhist Sanskrit [6]. The above conclusion has also been drawn by other scholars [7]. The *stūpa* has also been considered as a 'relic shrine' and its origin has been traced to the ancient burial practices [8]. Taking into account the architecture of the surrounding railing and the actual ritual of veneration, it has been suggested that the origin of *stūpa* could be traced to pre-Buddhistic solar cult [9]. A long discussion on the issue has already been done[10] of which the most probable theory is as observed — 'the hemispherical structure emerged out of the earthen funeral mounds (*smaśānas*)' [11].

So far as early Buddhism was concerned, Gautama Buddha himself is said to have told Ananda, his most favorite disciple, to erect ***stūpa*** for the Tathagata at four cross-roads [12]. May be for this, ***stūpa*** architecture became a relic-depository-monument almost immediately after the great demise of the Buddha. At the same time, it became a 'symbol of the last great event of the Buddha's life, viz., the *parinirvāṇa*' [13]. In course of time it became an embodiment of the 'Great Master' and the idea developed into a cult [14]. Thus, as it has been recorded immediately after the '*mahāparinirvāṇa*' of the Master, his relics were distributed among the eight claimants of Eastern India, which was the cradle land of Buddhism. The kings or chiefs of Rajagriha, Vaisali, Kapilavastu, Allakappa, Ramagrama, Vethadipa, Prava and Kusinagar equally distributed, of course after a quarrel, the relics among themselves [15]. Taking away the relics the kings and chieftens erected stupa keeping the shape of the relic within, at their respective capital cities. But when the Mauryas of Pippalivana entered the scene and asked for a share by that time the relic was already distributed. Realising this they took away the coals of the pyre and erected a *stūpa* over it at their capital city [16].

Thus began the long journey of the structural *stūpa* architecture in India. This activity instantly became a familiar tradition, which must have been in vogue even during the time of the Buddha [17]. Although thẹre are evidences of the existence of Jaina *stūpa* prior to the period of the, Buddha [18], the erection of the first eight *stūpas*, as stated above, was the beginning so far as Buddhism is concerned. The adherents of the Buddha took the lead in erecting the *stūpa* either within the cities or nearby in a larger scale. Here is a clear picture of association of the religious beliefs and practices with that of architectural edifices.

An examination of the excavated sites and the reports thereof have shown that the earliest *stūpas* were only of a low earthen mound as at Vaisali. The earliest *stūpas* were only 'unpretentious earthen barrows' and were not of monumental character [19]. Apart from the original eight *stūpas*, the *stūpa* at Kausambi, which was almost nearly contemporaneous, was erected within the city. This again shows the relationship of the *stupa* and the city which was based on certain religious consideration. In this context a reference to the Piprahwa *stūpa* is noteworthy. The said *stūpa*, situated in the district of Basti, Uttar Pradesh boardering Nepal contained the original relic of Gautama Buddha. The inscribed casket found after excavation, now preserved in Indian Museum, Calcutta, shows the names of *Sukriti* and *Bhakti*. The inscription also made a reference to the brothers, sisters and relatives of Sukriti and *Bhakti*. It seem that these people had inherited the relic of the Buddha and helped erect the *stupa*. Interistingly this *stūpa* has further been identified with the original *stūpa* at Kapilavastu and known as the *nirvāṇa stūpa* [20].

In early Buddhist religion and art, *stūpa* became a phenomenal object both as relic depository and as the very edifice of worship. However, the real impetous of a universal character was provided by the great king of the Mauryan dynasty, viz. Asoka. Asoka has been credited with the evolution and spread of the *stūpa* architecture throughout his kingdom. To give a new orientation and direction, he is said to have reopened the original seven *stūpas* and sharing the relic erected many thousands stupas at sacred places and cross roads [21]. The Mauryan emperor could not reopen the *stūpa* at Ramagrama in face of a strong opposition of their devoted guardians, the Nagas [22]. Asoka has also been further credited to provided us with the earliest inscriptional evidence when he caused to inscribe the word 'thube', i.e., *stūpa* in his inscription at *Nigaliva/Nigali Sagar*, thirteen miles to the north-west of Rumindei. This was his 15th regnal year in the place where Asoka caused to have reconstructed and doubled the *stūpa* of

Kanakamana also known as *Konagamana/Kanakamuni*, the twenty-fourth Buddha. The king, in his 20th regnal year, personally visited the site and set up an inscribed pillar recording the above information[23]. This important archaeological evidence provides us with a definite data relating to the evolution of *stūpa* architecture. Further it shows that the erection of *stūpa* in memory of earlier Buddhas was very much in practice.

Not only the relic of Gautama Buddha and that of the twenty-fourth Buddha was venerated by erecting *stūpas*, but also that of Buddha's favourite and close disciples. At Sanchi two *stūpas* have been found being dedicated to Sariputta and Maudgalayana. Gradually with the spread of Buddhist tradition also set into erect *stūpas* keeping the personal items used by the Buddha and his great disciples. As years passed the *stūpa* architecture become widely prevalent. With the spread of Buddhism the followers could not remain content only by building *stūpas*. From second century B.C. we find carved *stūpa* appearing on the gateways and railings of the *stūpas* at Bharhut, Sanchi and Bodhgaya. From the same period the western part of India became very active so far as the Buddhist rock-cut architecture is concerned. As a result a large number of caves hewned out of the living rock at various places. Large monastic establishment grew and dedicated to the Buddhist *Samgha*. Sites such as Bhaja, Kondane, Ajanta, Pitalkhora, Bedsa, Karle, Kanheri, Junar, Nasik etc. evolved into famous monastic complexes. Invariably each monastic complex was provided with one or more caityas, the worship places. In each Caitya a rock-cut *stūpa* was cut out at the center of the apse. Such a *stūpa* within the caitya is the object of worship. Within the rock-cut cave the monolith *stūpa* is a replica of the structural variety in the open. As observed, during the closing centuries of the pre-Christian era the *stūpa* became the nucleus of every monastic complex and was looked upon as 'the outward and visible manifestation of the faith[24].

With the spread of Buddhism the *stūpa* in a totally different conception started to be cut out. This type is known as votive *stūpa*, which is a replica and at the same time portable one. These votive *stūpas* were found abundantly at monastic establishments. Being dedicatory in nature these were associated with the rithal practices. Followers donated these *stūpas* to the monastic establishments in order to gain merit. This practice gradually became universal. The religious and ritualistic elements in this practice made it all the more popular. Thus, the *stūpa* architecture, which was originally a relic-depository and devotional monument underwent changes both in its conception and as well as in philosophy.

Of the aniconic representations of the Buddha, *stūpa* occupied a very prominent place in early Buddhist art. In its various types, viz., open-air-structural, carved types, monolithic types as in the case of caityas and *vihāra-caityas* and that of votive types; *stūpa* continued to dominate Buddhist religion and art. No other aniconic representation could evolve so prominently as that of the *stūpa*. Needless to point out it was very intimately connected with the religious ritual and symbolism. Till the introduction of the anthropomorphic forms of the Sakyamuni Buddha in the first century A.D., *stūpa* remained the single most impertant celifice, both architectually and philosophically, in early Buddhist art and religion.

References

1. Dutta, N., *et. al., History and Culture of Indian People*, Vol. II, Gen. Ed., R.C. Majumdar, 1968, p.391.
2. Radhakrishnan, S., *Indian Philosophy,* Vol. I, Delhi, 1989, p.588.
3. Chattopadhyaya, D.P., *Indian Philosophy,* N. Delhi, 1982, p.127.
4. Coomaraswamy, A.K., *History of Indian and Indonesian Art*, N. Delhi, 1972, p.31.

5. Saraswati, S. K., *et. al., History and Culture of Indian People* Vol. II, 1968, p.487.
6. Rhys Davids, T. W., *Buddhist India*, Delhi, 1993, p.77-78.
7. Marshall, J., *A Guide to Taxila*, Delhi, 1960, p. 99 fn. 1.
8. Goetz, H., *The Art of World (India)*. Bombay, 1959, p.42.
9. Rowland, B., *The Art and Architecture of India*, Penguin Books Ltd., 1977, p.79.
10. Pant, S., *The Origin and Development of the Stupa Architecture*, Varanasi, 1976, 155ff.
11. Saraswati, S. K., *ibid.*, p. 488.
12. Rhys Davids, T. W., *et. al., Sacred Books of the East*, XI, Oxford, 1981, p.93.
13. Coomaraswamy, *A. K., p.* 30.
14. Sarkar, H., *Studies in Early Buddhist Architecture of India*, Delhi, 1966, p. 4.
15. Marshall, J., *ibid.*, p. 98; Rowland, B., *Ibid.*, p. 77, Bapat, P. V., New Delhi, 1997, p.244-46.
16. Marshall, J., *A Guide to Sanchi*, Delhi, 1956, p. 151.
17. Coomaraswamy, A. K., *ibid,* Brown, P., *Indian Architecture,* Bombay, 1965, p.7.
18. Smith, V. A., *Jaina Stupa and other Antiquities of Mathura*, Delhi, 1901, p.13-15.
19. Ghosh, A., *The City in Early Historical India*, Simla, 1973, p.25-26.
20. Sircar, D.C., *Select Inscriptions*, Vol. I, Calcutta, 1942 no. 46; Pant, S., *ibid.*, p.98-99.
21. Kosambi, D. D., *The Culture and Civilization of Ancient India in Historical Outline*, N. Delhi, 1986, p.159.
22. Marshall, J., *A Guide to Sanchi*, Delhi, 1956, p.47.
23. Sircar, D. C., *ibid.*, p.71.
24. Marshall, J., *A Guide to Taxila*, Delhi, 1960, p.99.

Right to Die: Euthanasia in Greeco-Roman and Indian Tradition

18

Sabujkoli (Sen) Mitra

If I can choose between a death of torture and one that is simple and easy, why should I not select the later. If I know that I must suffer without hope of relief I will depart not through fear of pain itself but because it prevents all for which I would live" [Seneca, Lucious Annaeus, 4/1 BC-AD 65].

Problematic issue

Our thought on decision about life and death have totally changed in the twentieth century. The future historians might note the dates of some historical decisions taken by some countries. On 4th February 1993, Britain's High Court ruled that doctors could lawfully act to end the life of patients. That was a landmark judgment by Britain's House of Lords in the case of Tony Blands. Bland sustained brain damage after being crushed in a crowed of spectators at a football match in 1989, at Hillsborough football stadium in Sheffield. The brain damage left him permanently and irrevocably unconscious, what is now termed as Persistent Vegetative State [PVS]. PVS is not fatal; people like Bland can remain alive for thirty or more years. They are not brain-dead. In this way they are akin to infants born with anencephaly [absence of a brain] or with their cerebral cortex destroyed.

Bland's parents, who accepted that their son had ceased to exist in any real biographical sense, although his body remained alive, asked the English courts to declare that it would be lawful for medical staffs to withdraw feeding and other life sustaining measures so that their son would die. Eventually the House of Lords ruled unanimously that such a course of action would be lawful. The problem was, of course, that although Tony Bland has permanently ceased to have 'a life' in any meaningful sense, he was not dead and would not die unless the court permitted doctors to take steps to that end. In November 30, 1994, the Netherlands parliament finally put into law the guidelines under which the Dutch doctors are permitted to give lethal injections to patients who are suffering unbearably without hope of improvement, and who asked to help to die. Though in America there is no such law but on May 24, 1994 twelve Michigan jurors acquitted Dr. Jack Kevrokian of a charge of assistaining a man named Thomas Hyde to commit suicide. Their refusal to convict Kevrokian was a major victory for the physicians who were assisting patients to commit suicide. Because Kevrokian admitted supplying the carbon monoxide gas, tubing and a mask to Hyde, who had then used them to end a life made unbearable by a rapidly progressing nerve disorder known as A.L.S. .

However, the American medical association has a policy which says that a doctor can ethically withdraw all kinds of life prolonging treatments from a patient in an irreversible coma. But sticks to the law that "the physicians should not intentionally cause death". What a contradiction! The main question which bothers me is how can one, suffering from incurable disease end his life with dignity? To me, the only answer is Euthanasia, voluntary termination of life or "freedom to leave". We find these concepts in ancient Greece, Rome and in India also, though there were difference among them from social and spiritual point of view, one thing common to all of them was that it was closely associated with human dilemmas involved in advanced old age and severe illness. In classical Greece, the term Euthanasia meant "good death" (EU-good and thanatos-death) and referred primarily to the mode of dying, an easy and painless death. Greece had a rational attitude towards life; they did believe that all human life is precise and should be preserved at all costs. There was a generally recognized "freedom to leave" that permitted the sick and the despondents to terminate their lives, sometimes with outside help. Thus the ancient view of Euthanasia in these countries were close to suicide, which was voluntary self-imposed.

Euthanasia in Greeco Roman Tradition

It is possible to distinguish at least eight recurring types of suicide that were recognized in the Greeco-Roman period. What distinguishes them from each other is primarily available estimate of the supposed motives of the subject for taking leave from the world. It is suicide in the sense of a voluntary death (Mors voluntaria) that deserves our utmost attention here. We can divide the types of selfwilled deaths into two groups. Heroic suicide, characterized by the subjects desire to escape present or impending shame and dishonour or the noble wish to devote one's own life to one's country, second is nonheroic suicide, which by degrees only, tended not as a group to be inspiring to the ancients perhaps partly because they were perceived to be on the whole more epistemologically motivated or because they were thought to occur regularly in less glorious circumstances.

To the first heroic group belong four recurring cases motivated by[1] the desire to escape shame, dishonour,[2] the desire to demonstrate the total self-devotion to one's country[3] the desire to end unrelieved grief over the death of a loved one and[4] the desire to atone for the death one has accidentally caused to another person. To the second nonheroic group belong additional types of suicide motivated by[5] the desire to end personal grief owing to persistent and degrading poverty,[6] the desire to be united in death with a deceased lover one or companion, [7] the desire to quit life owing to the sheer sense of how boring, pointless, and futile it may appear, a motive which, significantly, it often redescribed as a form of madness, and finally[8] the desire to escape a relentless painful illness or infirmity, usually thought to be incurable in nature, and usually associated with the approach of the old age. This last type of suicide, which may call voluntary euthanasia is illustrated in the cases of elderly citizens of Ceos, who once, they became sixty, were in the habit of taking leave from life by drinking hemlock [often the doctors supplied the hemlock]. Also there is the case of Titus Aristo, who, carefully reasoned that he would end his life if his physicians reported that his insufferable illness was definitely beyond their means to cure.

In sum, it is to this second type of non-heroic suicide that voluntary euthanasia in most cases belonged. The case of Aristo and historical evidence about the possession of lethal drug by the ancient physicians point to the unique opportunity of the doctor to declare his patient untreatable, and, if requested, supply to his the appropriate "cup of death". This is an example of active/positive euthanasia. Beside the ever-popular hemlock, there were other methods also, such as self-immolation, jumping from high places, drowning, self-starvation hanging, running one self through by the sword or dagger. Moreover of these foregoing methods starvation can be compared to the passive euthanasia of modern times, wherein the patients death is brought about by omitting those elements necessary to the support of biological life. The others would qualify as active form of euthanasia, where in death occurs as the more immediate result of committing a fatal attack of some sort.

Let us turn to the ancient India.

Euthanasia in Indian Tradition

Death has been described as a central concern of Indian philosophy, religion and society. There are three basic types of death described in Indian philosophy, natural, unnatural [being killed], and self-willed [killing oneself]. With reference to natural death we find that there was a strong Brahmanical prescription to live hundred years at least to the end of natural life span. The funeral or sraddha rites were performed to those who died a natural death. Unnatural death being killed in a battle, by murder or by accident were viewed as accidents and not to be marked by a sraddha. Such deaths were not perceived always negatively. The death of a warrior killed in a battle was religiously powerful [for example, the death of Duryodhana, Karna, Meghnāda, Rāvana], for it leads to heaven or deification. Beside natural death and unnatural violent death, there also developed an acceptance of some sort of self-willed death. This self-willed deaths are of three different types. Suicide, voluntary death [Mors voluntaria heroica] and religious death [Mors voluntaria religiosa]. Suicide was self-willed death prompted by passion, depression, or uncontrollable circumstances, and it was prohibited. Heroic deaths were found mainly among the warriors of the ancient times. It was a way to avoid calamity [for example, jawahar brata of Rajasthan] when a person wanted to avoid capture, or a women wanted to avoid rape or slavery by a conqueror through self-willed death, it was a substitute for heroic death in battle that resulted in heaven. The religious death emphasized the religious dimension [heaven, liberation, dharma, duty and social order, based on religious principles].

Ātmahatyā or *ātamghāta* became the technical term for suicide in classical period. The heroic and religious deaths were known as, *icchārmrtyu*, *istatmrtyu*, *mahāprasthāna* [death while in mediation], prāyopovesana [abstaining form food and awaiting in a seating posture for the approach of death]. The Jaina equivalent to prāyopavesan is sallakhanā which is regarded as passive euthanasia practiced in ancient Indian. There are a number of descriptions of self-willed deaths in Indian tradition, such as sati, drowing in the river, jumping form the top of the hill etc.

It has been observed that much sympathy was expressed in classical India for euthanasia in the sense of "freedom to leave" by one suffering from seemingly incurable disease or by one facing debilitating old age. In the Manusmriti, discourse V, the bhasya by Medhatithi, verse 88, it is stated that" water offering is withdrawn from those.... who have abandoned themselves, i.e., those who even before their span has run out or given up their bodies. It was considered quite desirable in the case of old men suffering from incurable diseases given up by the physicians, as has been thus declared..." if an old man incapable of purification and memory, who has past beyond the reach of the physicians' art, kills himself by falling down from the precipice, or entering into fire or by fasting or by drowning into water..." Voluntary termination was regarded as desirable, also. In the cases of persons suffering from leprosy and such other diseases. It was also desirable to men who though still in the house holder's state, have lost all energy, bent upon entering the great path, they do not wish to live on uselessly. That man was called devoid of energy, who was incapable of doing purificatory acts, as also saying the twilight prayers etc. Again in Manu Samhita, it is said that, "if one whose body has been emaciated, or who has lost all his energy should kill himself, which means that voluntary termination was permitted in society for some people. So euthanasia in the sense of "freedom to leave" belonged to the category of self-willed death. Moreover, if once there was a public declaration of the intention to perform self-willed death, helping the person was allowed. In the events of Antarjali yatra, Ganga yatra, Mahaprasthana, members of the family and society used to help the person who wanted self-willed death. The individual's choice or will power was therefore, mandatory when euthanasia in the sense "freedom to leave" was accepted in the Indian society, till 18th century. Although there was positive evolution of "freedom to leave" in classical Hinduism, a strong criticism developed in the British period. Then, the Indian penal code, based on British law included all kinds of self-willed death and euthanasia in the sense of "freedom to leave" under a single term "suicide", which was and is still viewed as criminal act. So "freedom to leave" became illegal with the advent of British law in India.

A challenge to the Indian Penal Code's ruling on euthanasia was made by Minoo Masani and justice Tukol. Both of them strongly advocated for euthansia. Justice Tukol delivered a series of lectures under the title "Sallekhana is not a suicide". While commentators of Indian Penal Code have included the cases of, religious fasting to death among the forms of suicide, justice Tukol argued that sallekhana is note case of suicide. All the religions of Indian origin, the Jainas positively advocates euthanasia or self-willed death or sallekhana. The two verses of "*Ratna Karandaka Srāvakāchāra* [22'23], describe the Jaina cencept of voluntary death as legitimate responses to debilitating old age and incurable diseases.

> "*Upasarge durbhikse jarāsi rujāyām ca nihpratikāre*
> *Dharmayahtanvimochanamahu sallekhana marayah*".

The wise one says that sallekhana is giving up the body when there is calamity [*upasarga*], suffering from famine [*durbhikses*], old age and decay [jarasi], painful disease [ruja] and incurable disease [*nihpratikāre*] for the sake of *dharma*.

and

Antahkriyadhikaranam tapah phalam Sakaladarsinah stuyate Tasmad yavad bibhavamsamadhi marane Prayatitavyam".

All systems of religions praise the result of austerities [tapah], which is control of mind and action, therefore, one should attain emancipation from existence [*bibhava*] in *samadhimarana*.

The Jains have suggested the ways of discarding life in exceptional cases or situations. It is very interesting to note that the philosophy, whose fundamental principle is non-violence [*ahimsa*] puts forth a systematic theory of accepting death peacefully and voluntarily.

Every Jaina has to follow the rules known as *anuvratas sallekhana* or *santhara* are anubratas, i.e. practice. There are many examples of Jaina monks who have accepted death by taking *santharavrata*. According to Uttrahdhyāna Sutra, there are two types of death; accepting death without fear and accepting death with fear and reluctance. In the first case, the man has a control over death and this type of death is called *samādhimarana* or *pandita marana*. Here the person understands the art of "non-attachment". The Jaina scriptures mentions certain conditions, when all the organs of the body become just like a skeleton, due to incompetence one can not perform the religious and social duties, then one is allowed to prefer *santhara*.

Conclusion

Death is a part of life, as necessary as sleep. So the wise men should not have an anxiety regarding death. But the fact that what worries man is not the fact of dying, but the manner of dying, painful death or being alive with incurable disease, suffering for a long time or being persistant, vegetative state. So as long as the body is useful, it should be maintained, when the body becomes helpless in performing necessary duties it should be thrown away. The final decision should be taken by the person concerned. This view requires a great kind of self-control. According to it the life that has a sancity is not a helpless life but is a qualitively better life, based on obligation to the community and society. Apart from Jainism we also find some similar views in Hindu sastras. P.V.Kane in his "*History of the Dharma Sastras*", writes that "...but Atri states some exception namely, if one who can not observe the rules of bodily purification [owing to extreme weakness], one who is so ill that no medical help can be given, kills himself in the precipice or into the fire or water or by fasting till death, mourning should be observed for him for three days and Srāddha may be performed for him...." Aprarka quotes the texts of Brahmagarbha, Vivasvat and Gargya about a householder: "...he who is suffering from serious illness, or who is very old, who had carried out his task, may bring about death at pleasure by resorting to Mahaprasthana, by entering into either fire/water or by falling from a precipice. By doing so he incurs no sin and his death is far better than Tapas". This is clear that the Brahmin authors in no uncertain terms, accepted the practice of active euthanasia. It seems that at that time no lethal injections were available, so they had to choose the crude ways for termination of life.

Caraka Samhitā also discusses the concept of death, though in different context and from different angle. It discusses the duties and conduct of a physician in dealing with a patient whose death is inevitable. Caraka gives a detail account of rstalaksana in the section called indriyasthāna of the Caraka samhita. It is stated that when a physician will notice about the inevitable and imminent death of a patient, he should not declare it to the dying person, which may be disastrous to the patients or to the family members. Without disclosing anything he should refrain from treating the patient.

Caraka Pandita explains, this kind of patient, whose death is imminent should be ignored, that is, he should not be given medicine because there is a fear of losing one's reputation [yasohanādibhayat]. This is nothing but passive euthanasia.

Before concluding, I would like to say that, we, the human beings have a right over own body. We have a right to live with dignity and also we have a right "to leave" with dignity. When the quality of life comes to be questioned, there, 'I', should be the authority to take decision on 'my' life. And when the dignified ways of accepting death were already practiced throughout the ages in India, the legalization of active euthanasia can not be and should not be a problematic issue in India.

References

1. *Routledge Encyclopedea of Philosophy*, General Editor, Edwards Caig, Routledge, London, New York, 1998, p.627.
2. "Active and passive Euthanasia", James Rachel, in the New *England Journal of Medicine*, Vol.292, 1975, p-78-80.
3. 'Euthanasia', Helga Kushe, In a Companion to Ethics, ed. by Peter Singer, Blackwell, 1993.
4. "Rethinking Life and Death" Practical Ethics, Peter Singer, Oxford University Press, 1994 see Margoli's Negatives, Chap. II, "Sucide".
5. Ethical Issue in Death and Dying, Prentice Hall, New Jersey.
6. Hindu Ethics, Purity Abortion and Ethanasia, J. Lipner, Catherine Young and H. Coward, United States Publishing House, 1993.

7. History in the Study of Suicide, Rosem George "Psychological Medicine", 1, 272, 1971.
8. The Law of Manu, Manusmrti with bhasya by Meedhatithi, translation by Ganganath Jha, Vol. III, Calcutta University, 1922.

Bibliography

1. *Purusarthasidhyucharya*, Sri Amrita Chandracharya, Sri Parausruta Pravavak Mandal, Agra 1966.
2. *History of Dharmasastras*, P.V. Kane, Bhanderkar Oriental Institute, Pune, 1974.

Relevance of Buddhism and other Religions in Modern Society

19

G. C. Nayak

Religion, as a phenomenon, is so very near, so very intimate, to all of us that even when we try to avoid religion, in some form or the other, it tends to cling to us in some other form and even when we deliberately try to cultivate an anti religious or an irreligious stance, religion does not leave us even for a moment, so to say, because it seems to be here, there, and every where starting us in our face, whether we like it or not, its all-encompassing embrace.

On the other hand, religion appears to be so very remote, so very far from us, in as much as a sort of intransigent mystery seems to be lying at the very heart of its being since the time immemorial; in its multifarious aspects and multi-dimensional forms, it continues to remain somewhat baffling even for the best of the human intelligence, to say the least. This bafflement has been evident even in our earliest thoughts. The deep sense of mystery expressed in inimitable literary style of the Ṛgvedic 'Hymn to creation' is the earliest example available to us, displaying the characteristically unfathomable nature of creation and the creator which traditionally constitute the subject-matter of religion. "Who truly knows", asks the Vedic sage, "and who can declare it? Whence it was born, and how this world was fashioned? The gods came later than the earth's creation: who knows then out of what the world has issued? Whether he made the world or did not make it. He knows whence this creation came. He only who in the highest heaven guards and watches: He knows indeed, but then, perhaps. He knows not!"

This is true not only of any specific topic or subject of religion but of religion as a phenomenon on the whole. Naturally and quite understandably, therefore, I shall be proceeding to deal with this topic with utmost humility and caution.

Moreover, there is another problem worth noting here. If one seeks to arrive at a definition of what religion is, it won't be possible for him to find one which should be acceptable to all religious sects and denominations. Perhaps Wittgenstein's famous notion of "family resemblance," of "similarities crisscrossing and overlapping" may be of some help here. For an adequate assessment of the situation one may be required to concentrate on what is popularly understood to be a religious way of life. As Professor H.D. Lewis has aptly observed in his *Philosophy of Religion*.

"It is not difficult to anticipate what the word 'religion' would first call to mind for readers of this book. They would probably associate it, in the first place, with certain kinds of buildings called 'acts of' worship that go on there. Closely allied to this is the role of persons specially appointed and instructed to take a leading part in these performances, priests and preachers. These are known to wear special kinds of clothes, sometimes because that is involved in the part they play in acts of worship and sometimes as a general indication of their office and the way it is thought of by themselves and other members of the community. In the first case we have vestments of various kinds and in the second the round collar and the rather somber cloth of the clergy. These have their well-known equivalents in religions other than the Christian one."

Religion as a phenomenon involving the sense of the sacred, "the idea of the holy", "a way of valuing most comprehensively and intensively", religious valuing as "something involving ultimate concern" are only various examples of sophisticated understanding of the religious way of life.

In the modern society, the pride of place mostly goes to scientific temper and secularism, no doubt but at the same time it needs to be noted that religion has not become redundant or irrelevant for that very reason. World-religions like Hinduism, Christianity, Islam, Sikhism, Buddhism and Jainism, for example, have not only not lost their relevance and importance in the present-day society, but it is also evident that they are growing from strength to greater strength alongside our scientific temper and secularist outlook. It is remarkable indeed, and there must be some reason for this. These world religions have a very significant role to play even in the modern society influenced largely by the scientific temper and secularist spirit.

'Secularism' is a term which has aroused a lot of controversy and confusion among scholars because of its diverse implications and different meanings attached to the term in different contexts. The term 'secular' has been used primarily in a sense opposed to the 'religious', 'other worldly', 'spiritual' and 'sacred'. One need not go into the history of how this term came to be used in the sense of 'anti-religious' or 'irreligious' in the first instance. The Latin term 'Saeculum' which means 'the age, the world' may throw some light in this regard. According to Hackman, "secularism signifies the kind of life that is lived in complete indifference to God and to religious values"[1]. It has been taken to mean not only some thing "non-spiritual, having no concern with religious or spiritual matters"[2], but also "a movement, intentionally ethical, negatively religious with political and philosophical antecedents"[3]. It has also been taken to be "an attempt to establish an autonomous sphere of knowledge purged of supernatural, fideistic presuppositions"[4]. From this point of view certain point of contact between secularism and scientific temper is quite discernible. According to new begin, "the true secularism has been taken to refer to a system of belief or an attitude which in principle denies the existence or the significance of realities other than those, which can be measured by the methods of natural science"[5]. Scientific temper stands for an attitude of mind that does not take into account any thing other than that which is conducive to the search of knowledge. As Russell has aptly remarked, "The scientific attitude of mind involves a sweeping away of all other desires in the interests of the desires to know"[6]. "The kernel of the scientific out look", according to him, is "the refusal to regard our own desires, tastes and interests as affording a key to the understanding of the world"[7].

The question, however, is whether religion can be ignored altogether in favour of the scientific temper or the secularists spirit. Supposing that religious or spiritual matters need to be properly apprehended in the course of our search for knowledge or truth, supposing that they are matters of importance in our search for knowledge of the world as a whole, it may so transpire that by ignoring these matters our genuine search for knowledge would be vitiated or misguided to that extent. At least a religious person would think it to be so. If religion is ignored, or if there is a deliberately anti-religious trends associated with secularism. Is it not itself unscientific? Are we do justice to all aspects of life if in our search for truth or knowledge we ignore one of the most vital aspects, viz. the religious one? As Tallish points out, "Religion opens up the depth of man's spiritual life which is usually covered by the dust of our daily life and noise of our secular work. It gives us the experience of the holy, of some things which is untouchable, awe-inspiring, an ultimate meaning, the source of ultimate courage. This is the glory of what we call religion"[8]. Here one must be very careful. There is form of secularism in which a secular man, though not himself religious, is expected not to ignore religion altogether. He may be a respecter of different forms of religious life with a detached look. On the other hand, even if he in his own private life subscribes to one of the various religious forms, he may, in so far as he has a secular outlook, develop respect for the other forms and have a detached and impartial out look towards all religions.

But is not religion necessarily dogmatic and hence not amenable to an open discussion? As Russell points out, "The world needs open hearts and open minds, and dit is through rigid systems, whether old or new, that these can be derived"[9]. But why should religion be identified with dogmas? Can one not be regarded as religious, even truly religious in certain contexts, although he may not subscribe to any of the specific dogmas? This is a very important question to which any answer whatever may appear to be controversial, for it depends so much on different perspectives and understanding. But to me it appears that we can conceive of a truly religious way of life devoid of dogmas. Dogma, though not very unfamiliar in religion, is certainly not intrinsic to it.

'Dogma' here is used to signify dogmatism in some form or the other and this is the sense in which 'dogma' is not intrinsic to religion, although it is true that one cannot be called religious without commitments of some sort or the other. It is high time that we may back even in connection with the word 'love', an apparently loveable english word. It is no wonder if the word 'dogma' with its pejorative association of 'dogmatic' should be considered an anathema in religion where dogmatism cannot be considered to be virtue in any case.

It is the commitment to that which is supposed to be the highest, the best, the Paramartha, which is the most fundamental aspect of religion, not its dogmatism. Dogmatism leads to bigotry, intolerance and a sort of maniacal conduct on the part of one who is wedded to such dogmas, whereas a particular commitment to that which is the highest or the best may make room for or at least permit a meaningful dialogue with other sincere and serious commitments not only without risking its own cause but also with positive purpose or promoting its cause in a larger context. Hence I would advocate the cause of religion without dogma only in this sense, not in the sense of religion as devoid of its sincere and fundamental commitments which would certainly be a contradiction in terms. My point is that there is no reason why one cannot lead a truly religious life devoid of dogmas and why religious questions cannot be discussed with scientific temper.

I will be exploring here the possibility of arriving at a certain consensus regarding the minimum that is common almost all the world-religions irrespective of any specific dogma which might lead to bigotry and intolerance. Each of the world-religions has its own specific features no doubt, but as religious phenomenon they also possess certain common features which need to be highlighted.

In religion we encounter an unique phenomenon of a total commitment and dedication to that which is considered to be the highest and the best along with a need to uplift the humanity at large in the direction of that highest goal. That is why, religion is supposed to fulfil the inner most urge of man. I am of course not referring here to the aberrations of religion which might have played havoc at times in the history of mankind. A truly religious man it glided and inspired by what I would call a "unique concern for the weakling," a concern for all those who are weak in some respect or the other. The entire life of a truly religious man it orientated towards the alleviation of the sufferings of the weak[10]. Different typed of weakness may be found in different persons, groups or nations which need eradication at the hands of a truly religious man. Such persons or groups may belong to the rich or poor, the learned or the illiterate and even the powerful or the powerless. The concern of the truly religious man is with the common weaknesses and drawbacks which cause untold suffering to the humanity at large, and this is the sense in which I have designated it as a "concern for the weakling". A king from this point of view may be considered a weakling in a certain contest and may benefit immensely from the contact of a truly religion man. The life-history of Ashoka may be cited as a case in point. This "concern for the weakling" seems to be a whole-time passion with the religious man. The only thing which needs to be remembered in this connection is that the term "weakling" here does not refer to a specific class of persons, groups of nations. The reference is to the human weakness, wherever and in whatever form it may be found, even despite appearances to the contrary in certain contexts. One may, to all outward purposes, appear to be quite strong otherwise, but at the same time he or she may very miserably be lacking only in strength of character, a person about whom The Bible would say, "What is a man profited, if he shall gain the whole world, and lose his own soul?" Physically, mentally as well as spiritually weak and distressed persons, groups or societies receive the primary attention of the religious man because of his genuine love for them for whose alleviation of suffering his message of what he considers to be the best, the *Paramartha*, is meant. This may be regarded as a sort of therapeutic conception of religion[10A]. This is the sense in which God has been regarded as "Dinabandhu" (a friend of week) in Hinduism and Guru Nanak has declared that he is a friend of the lowliest ("*Nica anadari nica jati nicihu ati nicu, Nanaku tin kai sanga sathi badia siu kya ris*"). Buddha's Mahakaruna also points in the same direction. Jesus, the Son of God, of the Bible is well-known to have a definite soft corner for the "weakling" and prophet Mohammed's concern for the poor and the weak is no less conspicuous. Vivekananda, one of the great modern exponents of Hinduism, is known to have given a call to treat the poor and the illiterates as the objects of veneration (*Daridra devo bhava, murkha devo bhava*)[11]. This is a regular feature, I should think, of the world-religions which needs to be highlighted. The concern for the weak in the religious man seems to find its inspiration from his realisation that he has encountered or apprehended the highest and the best in his life that this unique experience needs to be shared with others who are less fortunate. It is significant that these features are found both in Godless religions and religions having faith in different types or Divinity or Godhead in the context of the world-religions. The problem of dealing with the weakling with a genuine concern for his or her welfare has always been no doubt, but it has been much more urgent in the modern society because of highly subtle and sophisticated ways and means by which exploitation of one another works in the present day society, and the task of truly religious person has therefore become much more relevant, much more urgent, in the modern society.

A typically dedicated life with its own belief-systems and commitment to the best, the *Paramartha*, along with a unique concern for the weak can be regarded as truly religious, according to me, irrespective of any particular type of belief, dogma, and worship which may or may not form an integral part of such a life. Lives of great religious saints, irrespective of the place or time to which they may belong, can be cited as exampled in this regard. But could it not be construed as a mere stipulation, persuasion or even a sort of imposition from my side and for that matter from the side of any of those who would subscribe to this view? Well, I do admit that it could be construed as a stipulation or persuasion, but it is not necessary that it should be so. I would like to submit for consideration is that there is a definite use in the sense mentioned above of the word "religious" or "religion" which is available to us and it would therefore not be wrong if this idea is highlighted in religion irrespective of the exact nature of its external wrappings or its specific dogmas.

"The plain fact", as William James has pointed out with a reare insight into the subject, "Is that men's minds are built, as has been often said, in water-tight compartments. Religious after a fashion, they yet have many other things in them beside their religions, and unholy entanglements and associations inevitably obtain. The baseness so commonly charged to religion's account are thus, almost all of them, not chargeable at all to religion proper, but rather to religion's wicked practical partner, the spirit of corporate dominion. And the bigotries are most of them in their turn chargeable to religion's wicked intellectual partner, the spirit of dogmatic dominion, the passion for laying down the law in the form of an absolutely closed in theoretic system. The ecclesiastical spirit in general is the sum of these two spirits of dominion[12]". Though there is no doubt some truth in what William James has said, it is, however, only a partial truth. Instead of putting the entire blame at the door of the ecclesiastical spirit, one should take note of certain intrinsic features of religion proper and a possible infiltration of bigotry in and through those very features. It seems to be a significant feature about religion that there cannot be a religion without a total commitment or devotion to that which it considers to be the highest and the best. It is therefore nothing strange or extra-ordinary that a religious person or an Institution should have his own total commitments. Own such commitment or devotion may have its origin in some such Gospel as that of Mark, "Thou shalt love the Lord thy God with all thy heart, and with all thy soul, and with all thy mind, and with all thy strength," and another may get its inspiration from the teachings of Sri Kṛṣna in the Bhagavadgita to take resort to Him, forsaking all considerations of *dharma* (sarva dharman parityajya mamekam saranam braja). Even one may be said to be committed to tolerance, to the point of view that all the different parts of different religions lead to the same goal, as evinced in "Reinam vaicitryad etc" of the *Śiva mahima*, or on the other hand one may be committed exclusively to one particular path. One may, while avoiding commitment to all dogmatic theories as Nagarjuna does, be viewed as being wedded to such a non-commitment. In this sense the life of a truly religious man is a typically dedicated life; there is not only concern here, there is an ultimate concern without which it cannot be regarded as religious. This ultimate concern, total commitment or a typical dedication to its cause can easily make room for and be confused with bigotry, although bigotry is not the same as dedication or commitment. It is of seminal importance therefore that this subtle distinction should not only be made in our day-to-day religious practice, but it should also be highlighted. From the ultimate concern of the religious man it does not follow that he must be a bigot and promote bigotry, and further it does not follow from the commitment that the religious man or institution cannot allow an open discussion on the subject. Can't we agree to differ afterall? The point is that within the framework of different religious commitments there can be mutual understanding and harmony; irrationality and Pig-headedness are not the necessary concomitants or outcome of different commitments. An open-minded approach need be and ought not to be sacrificed at the altar of bigotry and irrationality in the name of commitment. There can be discussion with "open hearts and open minds" in inter-religious circles also, provided the distinction between religious commitment and religious bigotry is clearly brought out. What I mean to say is that religions along with their different commitments can be discussed with a scientific temper, provided we are prepared to face the commitments of different religions with tolerance and mutual respect for each other.

For my part, I consider it is to be inbuilt in the very structure of the world-religions that they may not only come to a clash with each other, as they have done from time to time on account of the clinging to dogmas of different sorts, but they can also try to understand with sincerely each other's commitments in the interest of human welfare which has been the genuine concern at least of the masters themselves like Buddha, Christ, Mohammed, Nanak and Sri Kṛṣna, to name only a few leaders, who are responsible for giving flesh and blood to these religions.

In this connection Buddha has set an ideal before us in propagating a religion that is committed to freedom from dogmas through analysis and thus being conducive to the welfare of the humanity at large (Bahujana sukhāya, bahujana hitāya)[12a]. I place it before the learned readers only as an example of a religious phenomenon parexcellence alongwith its development in the direction of *Madhyamika Sunyavada*.

There is hardly any parallel in the history of mankind to Buddha's avoidance of dogmas through analysis as evidenced in Sutta 63 of the Majjhima Nikaya and his persistent refusal to be swayed away be any dogmatic view whatsoever, e.g. in the Sutta-Nipata:

"From lusts and dogmas free, quit too of theories, he (unheeding sage) goes his stainless way, devoid of self-reproach" says the Lord.

A unique insight that steers clear between the extremes of rival theories by the help of analysis was in ample evidence in the method adopted by Buddha in his teachings. And it seems to have reached its culmination in Nagarjuna whose *Mūla-Madhyama-karika* along with its commentary *Prasannapada* by Candrakirti are landmarks in this direction.

In order to comprehend the immense significance of this insight the notion of *prajñaparamita* as the culmination of such a unique insight needs elucidations. For a correct assessment of the exact implication of the *Prajñaparamita*, however, and understanding of the concept of *pratityasamutpada* is a necessary prerequisite.

A unique conceptual revolution is launched by the *Mȧdhyamikas* in the philosophical firmament by a revealing, and consequently a novel, insight into the nature of *pratitya samutpȧda* which is one of the most fundamental, rather the key, concept of Buddhism. It is identified with *śunyatā* which in its turn is identified with *nihsvabhāvatā* and also with the *madhyamapratipad*, thus making the entire Buddhist thought appear as one systematic and harmonious whole with a central message of its own, which, to be precise enough, is not a message but a paradigm of wisdom. It does not imply the sequence of entities between which there is a casual relation; it points to the dependence of concepts upto one another. This mutual interdependence of concepts is, according to Nagarjuna, the *asme sa sunyatā* which is nothing but *nihsvabhāvatā*, that is essencelesness of the concepts. If every concept is dependent on another for its intelligibilty, how can it be said to have a fixed essence of its own? Own who understands *pratityasamutpadas*, that is mutul dependence of *parasparapeksa* of concepts, therefore, understands that they are all *śunya* or *nihsvabhāva*, i.e. they do not have an independent and permanent essence of their own. This is what Buddha means by *madhyamapratipad* also according to Nagarjuna, in as much as the relisation of the sunyata or *nihsvabhāvatā* or essencelessness of concepts steers clear between extremes or specultative metaphysical positions regarding the *svabhāva* or the fixed nature of things and thus makes one adopt a middle course amongst the contending metaphysical theories.

Freedom from contending metaphysical theories is one of the essential features of philosophical insight (*prajñā*) according to Nagarjuna who is only following Buddha's teaching to its logical conclusion. The insight in question become possible, however, through a realisation that there is no essence to hang upon or to cling to in ordinary discourse which is merely conventionally useful. Once this dawns upon the wise man, he desists from committing those errors which an essentialist or '*svabhāvavādi*' is likely to commit. '*Prajñā*' consists in the insight that makes us free from the bondage of essentialist picture-thinking (*sarvakaipanaksayarupa*), and Nirvana is nondifferent from this critical insight 'par excellence' which is free from essentialist picture-thinking.

'*Śunyatā*' stands for a denial of all metaphysical constructions and it is therefore strange that this in its turn be misrepresented as either a metaphysical decrine of 'Vo!d' or of the 'Absolute'. Buddhist thought is out and out anti-metaphysical and anti-speculative in its character and whose ever converts *Śunyatā* itself into a metaphysical doctrine of nihillsm or Absolutism or any thinking of the sort is declared by Buddha to be incurable, says Nagarjuna in one of his Karikas[13], *śunyatā sarva dstinam prokta nihsaranam jinain, yesām tu śunyatā drsistansadhyanvabhasine*. Candrakirti, whose commenting on this Karika, refers to Buddha's instructions to Kasyapa as follows: "O Kasyapa, it would be better to entertain the substance-view (*Pudgala dṛṣti*) of the magnitude of mount Sumern than to hug the *śunyatā* view of the nihilist (*abhavabhinivesinah*); I call him incurable who clings to *śunyatā* itself as a theory. If a drug administered to patient were to remove all his disorders but were to foul the stomach itself by remaining in it, would you call the patient cured? Even so, *śunyatā* is an antidote to all dogmatic view, but if a man were to cling to it for ever as a view itself, he is doomed'. Nagarjuna's critical insight consists in a consistent denial of all 'isms' and this is what is known as *Prajñā paramita* or wisdom parexcellence in *Mahāyāna* literature. A rare insight which consistently tried to avoid all sorts of dogmatic speculations by pointing out that '*nirvana*' consists in total annihilation of all *Kalpanas* or thought-constructions and speaks of Tathagata as one who is never engaged in thought constructions is reduced to the sad plight of becoming a victim of one or another *kalpana* or thought construction and the whole insight is thus lost in complete oblivion. As in the case of the nihilistic interpretation so also in the case of an absolutist or a transcendentalist approach to *śunyatā*, it is well to remand oneself of the following warning of Nagarjuna which has been conveniently overlooked and even forgotten, '*vinasayati durdṛṣta śunyatā mandamedha- sam, sarpo yatha durgrhito vidyava duspeasadhita*'[14]. Just as a snake caught in the wrong manner by a dull-witted person only caused death to him or as a magic wrongly employed destroys the magician, so also *Śunyatā* wrongly seen and understood only ruins the person concerned. Those who are observed with the idea of a positive entity or an absolute reality on the ground or basis of which everything is declared to be *śunya* are according to Chandrakirti like those persons who, when told that they well get nothing expect that 'nothing' will actually be given to them. *Yo na Kiñcidapi panyam dāsyānityukba sa ced dehibhestadeva mahyam na Kiñcinnāma panyamiti bruyāt sa kenopāyena sakyah panya bhāvam grahayitum*"[15]. The *tattva* or the *paramārtha* here, the ultimate, the highest and the best is said to be "*apara pratyayam sāntam prapañcairaprapancitam*". All these descriptions, however, do not apply to any Absolute transcending through nor do they refer to *śunyatā* in the sense of the void of nihilism; they are only the descriptions of the state of affair when one realises *śunyatā* in the sense of *nihsvabhāvatā* or essencelessness of everything, of all ideas or concepts, although they have their conventional or practical utility of course. As Nagarjuna points out, "*Dve satya samupasṛitya Buddhānām Dharma desanā. Loka samvriti satyam ca satyam ca paramārthatah. Yenayorna vijanati*

Vibhagam Satyayordvayoh, Te tattvam na vijananti gambhiram Buddha sasana"[16]. This is the great Buddhist insist. At the end of the Karika, Nagarjuna bows does to Gautama for giving this rare insight that eliminates all dogmas and dogmatic thought constructions through his teaching imparted out of *anukampā* or *Mahākarunā*.[17]

The insight has a far-reaching implication in the present day society, with all its so-called modern technology and scientific progresss, with all its professed secularism and scientific temper, is fraught with conflicts, dissensions and an overdoes of violence. *Śunyatā* as a form of life, understood and parctised in the right perspective both in the national and international level, can be conducive to the cessation of dogmatic clinging to the essentialist thought construction which is at the rot of the most of our man-made problems. And what is more, the *śunyatā*-realisation culminates in *Mahākaruna*; as *Prājna karamati* point out, "*Yathabhutadarsina Bodhisattvasya sattesu Mahakaruna pravartate*"[18]. There is a positive emphasis in this Bodhisattva tradition on the alleviation of the suffering of others, since Karna is the deciding factor here[19].

If this has been put practice at all as a tradition or even as an innovative experiment in any part of this little world of ours, one has to admit that it has not always been done in right earnest nor has it been the essential feature of the form of life of the majority or even of a large number of people. The world, it seems, has not yet been genuinely ready for this. As Sri Aurobindo has aptly pointed out in another context, "Teachers of the law of love and oneness there must be, for by that way must come the ultimate salvation. But not till the Time-spirit in man is ready, can the inner and the ultimate prevail over the outer and immediate reality. Christ and Buddha have come and gone, but it is Rudra who still holds the world in the hollow of his hand"[20]. Sincere effort in the positive direction, however, has to go on; the perspective of minority, even if it may have been so thought in the human history so far, may come to prevail in the long run some day as the right perspective after all, genuine as well as vigorous training-centres for this are the need of the hour.

Buddhism with its devise schools of thought is in exhaustibly vast and multi-dimensional in scope, and so also are after world-religions in their own way.

References

1. G.G.Hackman, *Relation in Modern Life* (Charles W. Kegley and Viljo Nikander, 1957) p.283.
2. *Encyclopaedia Britannica* (London, 1960) Vol. XX. p.264.
3. *Encyclopaedia of Religion and Ethics* (1954), Vol. XI, p.347.
4. *Encyclopaedia of the Social Sciences* (1048) VOL. XIII, p.631.
5. Leslie New begin, Honest Religion for Secular man. (Lucknow Publishing House, 1966) p.8.
6. B.Ressell, *Mysticism and Logic* (George Allen & Uniwin Ltd., 1963), p.38
7. *Ibid.*, p.37.
8. Paul Tillich, *Theology of Calcutta* (New York, 1959) p.9.
9. B.Russell, *Why I am not a Christian* (Simon and Schuster, 1957) Preface.
10. Cf. " Na Tvaham kamaya rejyam na svargam napunarbhavam, Kamaye duhkhataptanam praninamarttinasanam", whose the prayer is not for kingdom of heaven or even for emancipation from rebirth, but only for the eradication of the suffering of the distressed. Cf. also Bhima Bhoi, the great saint-poet of Orissa, "Praninka arata duhkha apramita dekhu dekhu keva sahu, Mo jivana pachhe narke padithau jagata uddara heu". "Let me suffer the torture of hell myself but let the whole of living creatures be liberated from suffering that is simply unbearable "world that are reminiseent of the Bodhisattva ideal of the Mahayana Buddhism.

10A. It is significant that the Lalita Vistara Speaks of the Buddha as the king of Physicians (Vaidyarat). Cr. "Cirature Jivaloke klesa-vyabhi-prapidite, vaidyarat tvam samutapannah sarva-vyadhi-pramocakah".

11. Cf. E.Ranade (compiler), *Swami Vivekananda's Rousing Call to Hindu Nation* (Centenary Publication, Calcutta, 1963) p. 93. As against the Darwinian theory of the '*Surval of the fittest*' the instruction given by Thankur Anukul Chandra, another spiritual leader of the modern times, to his privileged disciples is interesting and worthy of note. Cf. Roy Hauserman, Ocean in a Tea cup (Satsang Church, Calcutta-New York, Second Edition, 1977), p.327, "*Make the unfit fit*. Then we will all survive. Each man is a living universe. You cannot win words by losing so much".

12. W. James, *The Varieties of Religious Experience*, (The Modern Library, New York, 1929) pp. 330-31.

12A. Cf. Vinaya Pitaa, 1.23 "Caratha Bhikkhave, Carikam bahujanahitaya, bahujana sukhaya, lokanukampaya; athaya, hitaya, sukhaya, devamanussanam."

13. *Mula Madhayama Karika*, 13.8.

14. *Ibid.*, 24.11.

15. Prasannapada.

16. *Mulamadhyama karika*, 24.8 and 9.

17. Cf. *Ibid.*, 27.30, "Sarva drstiprahanaya yah saddharma madesayat, Aunkampamupadaya tam namasyami Gautamam". Cf. Majhima Nikaya "Atthi pana bho to Gotomassa kinci dihttgatam ti? Ditthigatam ti kho vatsa apamitam Tattagatassa"

18. Prajnakaramati, *Bodhicaryavatarapanjika*, 9.1.

19. *Ibid*. 8.103, "Karunaparatantrataya paraduhkhaduhkhinah sarvadukhuapaharanaya Yatnah". cf. Karuna as one of the noble virtues to be practised under Brahma vihāra Bhāvanā.

20. Sri. Aurobindo, *Essays on the Gita* (New York, 1950), p.343.

Contributors

1. **Dr. Ananda Sahoo** is a Reader in the Department of Ancient Indian History, Culture and Archaeology, Vidya-Bhavana, Visva-Bharati. His field of specialization is Art and Religion. Dr. Sahoo is credited with one book and many research articles.
2. **Dr. Arpita Chatterjee** is a scholar on Nepali, Tibetan and Buddhist Studies.
3. **Dr. Bimalendra Kumar** teaches Pali and Buddhist Studies at Banaras Hindu University, Varanasi. He has published several research papers on Buddhism.
4. **Dr. B.N. Banerjee** was the former Professor of the Department of Pali, Prakrit and Sanskrit, Visva-Bharati. At present he is the President of the Asiatic Society, Calcutta. Prof. Banerjee has been awarded by the President of India in recognition of his contributions in the field of Indological Studies in genetal and Sanskrit language and literature in particular.
5. **Dr. Rita Gupta** is the Professor of the Department of Philosophy and Comparative Religion, Visva-Bharati. Prof. Gupta is a well known scholar on Buddhist Philosophy.
6. **Dr. B.N. Mukherjee,** former Carmichael Professor of Ancient Indian History and Culture, University of Calcutta, is an eminent Indologist and scholar of Oriental Studies of India.

7. **Dr. C.S. Prasad,** an Alumni of Visva-Bharati, teaches Chinese language and literature at Nava Nalanda Mahavihara at Nalanda, Bihar. He was closely associated with Prof. Tucci.

8. **Dr. G.C. Nayak** was the former Professor of Philosophy in the Utkal University, Bhubaneswar. Professor Nayak also served the Sri Jagannath Sanskrit University for three years as its Vice-Chancellor. He is associated with many academic organisations.

9. **Dr. Kalpika Mukherjee** is the Professor of Sanskrit at Visva-Bharati.

10. **Dr. Indrani Das** teaches Italian language at Visva-Bharati, Santiniketan.

11. **Dr. Madhusudan Mallik** was the Professor of the Pali, Prakrit and Sanskrit at Visva-Bharati.

12. **Dr. Narendra Kumar Dash** is attached to the Department of Indo-Tibetan Studies at Visva-Bharati. He has published several books and research papers to his credit.

13. **Dr. Ram Singh Tomar** war the former Professor of Hindi, Visva-Bharati. He was closely associated with Prof. Tucci and IsMEO, the Institute established by Professor Tucci himself. Prof. Tomar was a Senior Ashramite of Santiniketan and an Emeritus Professor of Visva-Bharati.

14. **Dr. Sabuj Kali Mitra** is the Chairman of the Department of Philosophy and Comparative Religion, Visva-Bharati. Her field of specialisation is religion and Indian logic.

15. **Dr. Sabyasachi Bhattacharya,** former Vice-Chancellor of Visva-Bharati, is a reputed historian of India. Professor Bhattacharya is presently associated with the Department of History, JNU, New Delhi.

16. **Dr. Subrata Chakraborty** is the Professor in the Department of Ancient Indian History, Culture and Archaeology at Visva-Bharati. His field of specialisation is prehistoric Archaeology.

17. **Prof. Suniti Kumar Pathak,** a well known Tibetologist, was attached to the Department of Indo-Tibetan Studies, Visva-Bharati. He has published many books and research papers on Tibetan language, literature and culture.

18. **Dr. Pranabananda Jash,** Professor of the Department of Ancient Indian History, Culture and Archaeology, Visva-Bharati, is an eminent scholar on the religions and cultural history of India and Southeast Asia. Professor Jash has published many books and articles to his credit.

19. **Dr. Ujjvala Mazumdar,** Professor of Bengali, University of Calcutta, is a well known scholar of India.

Index

❑❑❑